Trade in Services and Developing Countries

ORGANISATION FOR ECONOMIC CO-OPERATION AND DEVELOPMENT

Pursuant to article 1 of the Convention signed in Paris on 14th December 1960, and which came into force on 30th September 1961, the Organisation for Economic Co-operation and Development (OECD) shall promote policies designed:

- to achieve the highest sustainable economic growth and employment and a rising standard of living in Member countries, while maintaining financial stability, and thus to contribute to the development of the world economy;
- to contribute to sound economic expansion in Member as well as non-member countries in the process of economic development; and
- to contribute to the expansion of world trade on a multilateral, non-discriminatory basis in accordance with international obligations.

The original Member countries of the OECD are Austria, Belgium, Canada, Denmark, France, the Federal Republic of Germany, Greece, Iceland, Ireland, Italy, Luxembourg, the Netherlands, Norway, Portugal, Spain, Sweden, Switzerland, Turkey, the United Kingdom and the United States. The following countries acceded subsequently through accession at the dates indicated hereafter: Japan (28th April 1964), Finland (28th January 1969), Australia (7th June 1971) and New Zealand (29th May 1973).

The Socialist Federal Republic of Yugoslavia takes part in some of the work of the OECD (agreement of 28th October 1961).

Publié en français sous le titre:

ÉCHANGES DE SERVICES
ET PAYS EN DÉVELOPPEMENT

The following report is based on OECD Secretariat papers prepared over a period of some two years as part of a programme of work on trade in services under the auspices of the Trade Committee.

Part I of the report considers the potential gains to developing countries from the liberalisation of trade in services, whether through increased export opportunities, as other countries' barriers are lowered, or through development gains, as reductions in local protection help promote both the efficiency of domestic resource allocation and the transfer of skills from overseas. Part II provides an elaboration of the adjustment process likely to be associated with trade liberalisation and the nature of developing country concerns which will need to be addressed in the course of liberalisation.

This report is published on the responsibility of the Secretary-General and does not necessarily reflect the views of Member governments.

Also available

NEWLY INDUSTRIALISING COUNTRIES. Challenge and Opportunity for OECD Countries (1988)
(70 88 01 1) ISBN 92-64-130041-1   150 pages   £11.00   US$20.00   FF90.00   DM39.00

STRUCTURAL ADJUSTMENT AND ECONOMIC PERFORMANCE (1988)
(03 87 02 1) ISBN 92-64-13006-3   372 pages   £19.50   US$39.95   FF195.00   DM84.00

THE EXPORT CREDIT FINANCING SYSTEMS IN OECD MEMBER COUNTRIES. Third Edition (1987)
(22 87 01 1)   ISBN 92-64-12947-2   286 pages   £11.00   US$22.00   FF110.00   DM49.00

COUNTERTRADE. Developing Country Practices (1985)
(22 85 02 1) ISBN 92-64-12746-1   40 pages   £4.50   US$9.00   FF45.00   DM22.00

AGRICULTURAL TRADE WITH DEVELOPING COUNTRIES (1984)
(51 84 02 1) ISBN 92-64-12579-5   114 pages   £5.60   US$11.00   FF56.00   DM25.00

Prices charged at the OECD Bookshop.

*THE OECD CATALOGUE OF PUBLICATIONS and supplements will be sent free of charge
on request addressed either to OECD Publications Service,
2, rue André-Pascal, 75775 PARIS CEDEX 16, or to the OECD Distributor in your country.*

TABLE OF CONTENTS

TRADE IN SERVICES AND DEVELOPING COUNTRIES

INTRODUCTION

Part I of this note considers the potential gains to developing countries (LDCs) from the liberalisation of trade in services, whether through increased export opportunities, as other countries' barriers are lowered, or through development gains, as reductions in local protection help promote both the efficiency of domestic resource allocation and the transfer of skills from overseas. Consideration is given also to the strains which a liberalisation process is likely to place on LDC economies. Finally, there is a brief discussion of the relative impact of liberalisation and adjustment on developing countries at markedly different stages of development. Individual sector experience of potential liberalisation gains, which provides the basis for the overall assessment, is outlined in Section B of Part I. There is, of course, an interrelationship between liberalisation gains from export opportunities and development gains reflecting increased efficiency. Increased efficiency in the allocation of domestic resources can feed back into increased export capacity. It is also true, however, that some, potentially distorting, policies of domestic support for indigenous service providers can contribute to export growth in the particular sector supported. Such policies may, nevertheless, contribute to overall inefficiency and costs to the economy as a whole. Hence, should developing country administrations consider that assistance to local service industries is warranted, it will be important that the form of support chosen is both temporary and has minimal distortive effects. This point will be reverted to throughout the paper.

It cannot be automatically assumed that the relatively favourable growth experience in the goods sector of developing countries with outward-oriented policies will necessarily be translated to services sector experience. Nevertheless, there is a presumption that reduced economic distortion in service activities and trade policies which provide similar incentives to production for the domestic and foreign markets would be reflected in more sustained growth and development and more resilience to external shocks. Moreover, it is arguable that, at least for some countries in some sectors, the particular characteristics of service activities may yield greater gains from trade expansion than are generally reflected in the goods sector (1).

The starting point for this assessment of potential liberalisation gains was a series of notes which sought to explore sectoral characteristics and the nature of LDC concerns related to trade in services. These sectoral studies have been incorporated in Part II. Part II thus provides an elaboration of the adjustment process described briefly in Part I. Adjustment is seen to reflect characteristics specific to individual sectors as well as two broad concerns which affect all service activities -- balance of payments strains at the macro-economic level and the impact on local service providers at the micro-economic level. It is evident that few, if any, of the concerns identified are unique to developing countries. It might be suggested, however, that the dependence and relative vulnerability of many developing countries renders these concerns more acute.

PART I: LIBERALISATION GAINS FOR DEVELOPING COUNTRIES

A. OVERALL ASSESSMENT

1. Liberalisation Gains

i) Export Opportunities

Those countries with viable service industries and an export capacity could expect to gain from a process of trade expansion. Some LDCs will be among those countries. Nevertheless, as noted in each of the sectors considered in Part II, the competitive position of developing countries in service activities is difficult to characterise. While it is generally considered that developed countries, overall, are likely to be more competitive than developing countries in most services, many LDCs will have a measure of competitiveness in certain areas of service activity.

Developing country competitiveness may reflect specific characteristics of the countries in question, whether in the form of national endowments -- such as physical and cultural resources or strategic location on international travel paths contributing to tourism potential -- or through special relations built up with other developing countries, a relevant factor in some intra-LDC trade in construction and engineering services. Other developing country export opportunities may arise from the attributes of particular sectors, whether in the form of declining entry costs in information, computer and communications (ICC) services as advances in microelectronics reduce the costs of communications; requirements for "mature" technology, as in construction services, where many developing countries have direct, practical experience; or opportunities for niche markets such as the US "offshore office" operations associated with data processing in the Caribbean. Underpinning many of these opportunities and of overriding importance for many developing countries is the element of competitiveness that is associated with labour-intensity. In some cases -- though not all, as seen below -- strength in labour-intensive sub-sectors may reflect a genuine comparative advantage in the sector as a whole and the basis for potential international competitiveness in that sector. A trade expansion process could help stimulate a fuller realisation of this potential. A wide range of services have specific areas requiring labour-intensive inputs: the distribution side of banking and financial services; some hotel operations in tourism; operational aspects of construction and engineering services. Moreover, some discrete service activities might be regarded as being predominantly labour-intensive. This applies, in particular, to areas of ICC services such as data processing, data input and software production.

While comprehensive data are lacking, an indication of the revealed comparative advantage of certain developing countries is evident over a wide spectrum of service sectors or sub-sectors where they have a growing, albeit modest, role. As seen in more detail in Section B, this role is not confined to activities such as construction and engineering, already widely acknowledged, but extends, for example, into computer services, international banking and professional services. It should be noted, however, that any assessment of developing (or developed) countries' underlying competitiveness as service exporters is complicated by the resort to Government support whether through subsidy or other forms of assistance. Forms of support are highly diverse and by no means equal in their distortive effect. Examples of government assistance are widespread in the areas of tourism, construction and engineering services, and in maritime transport. In the latter area three LDCs have been identified as having a revealed comparative advantage far above the level that would be expected on the basis of their relative factor endowments; government subsidy and protective cargo reservation measures are widespread in all three countries.

Given the nature of factor endowments in many developing countries, the question of factor mobility in services trade assumes considerable importance. The realisation of developing countries' export potential in services will depend, in large measure, on the scope for acknowledgement within a services framework of the need for service-provider mobility in the form of temporary relocation of essential personnel. Moreover, for individual developing countries the realisation of potential comparative advantage and the attainment of international competitiveness is subject to constraints, additional to any explicit barriers such countries may face in gaining market access.

-- In those areas where economies of scale are important, new entrants (including many LDCs) may find it difficult to attain an optimal level of operations. This is illustrated by the case of insurance where many developing country markets do not produce enough income to allow sufficient spread. In such circumstances, regional cooperation among developing countries may yield significant benefits.

-- Most, if not all, service activities which are relatively labour-intensive are likely also to have important skill- and capital-intensive aspects. Examples include electronic information networks in tourism, sophisticated machine-testing of computer software, and the development of multimodal transport as technological adaptation to container vessels facilitates the movement of goods by more than one transport mode. While some developing countries are able to sustain research and development (R&D) expenditure necessary to master the skills required, others may find that technological change is undermining the basis of their (labour-intensive) competitiveness. It should be noted that where economies of scale and R&D considerations are important -- helping first entrants to maintain their competitive edge -- the attainment of comparative advantage as part of a dynamic process may be rendered more difficult. Should industry support be considered warranted in these circumstances, the costs of such support would be correspondingly high.

-- Finally, the realisation of potential comparative advantage is likely to depend on considerations other than resource endowments and factor allocation. In particular, it may depend on market structure within the sector concerned. The fear has been expressed that, in certain circumstances, liberalisation could lead to a diminution of competition where dominant firms are able to engage in anti-competitive pricing behaviour. It has not been possible to document the extent of such a risk in practical terms -- a risk which, in any event is not of exclusive interest to developing countries.

While these constraints do not provide an argument against liberalisation -- indeed they may favour certain forms of liberalisation that promote skills transfer -- they serve as a reminder that LDC export opportunities, however real, should be seen in perspective.

ii) Development Gains

Policies which seek to protect indigenous service providers, limiting market access by foreign firms, are likely, in each of the sectors examined, to reduce the quality of the service on offer, whether, for example, by narrowing the range of available financial services and inhibiting the mobilisation of savings, delaying payment of insurance indemnities, or increasing shipping costs. Moreover, because of the extensive linkages (backward and forward) between particular service activities and other areas of economic activity the inter-sectoral costs of protection could be considerable. Policies which restrict the operations of foreign service providers, although they may raise the incomes of local sellers, act as a tax on local buyers -- buyers for whom, in most cases, the service is an input to the production, and export, of other goods and services (2). The efficiency of the agricultural sector, for example, is likely to depend importantly on financial services necessary for the realisation of production potential, on tourist consumer needs, on the level of shipping freight rates and on the information services necessary for effective response to changing market conditions.

The extent of efficiency gains for developing countries will depend, in part, on the level and nature of their protective barriers and the consequential distortions which these entail. Comprehensive information is lacking with respect to the level of service sector protection in developing (and developed) countries, particularly with respect to the relative level of protection in the services and goods sectors which has implications for general equilibrium analysis of liberalisation gains and shifts in relative prices. Nevertheless, there is evidence in most sectors that the level of LDCs' barriers to services trade, whether cross-border or establishment-based, is sufficiently high to provide ample scope for potential gains in efficiency (see Part II). This is not to deny that developing country regulations may be relatively limited in the area of consumer protection or in respect of rapidly evolving service activities dependent on high technology.

Given the pace of technological change and its impact on developing countries the most important benefit, over the longer-term, of a trade liberalisation process is likely to be the transfer of skills which frequently is associated with foreign-based service activities. This may come in various forms: as technology embodied in the service provided, through formal training programmes or through the flow of staff from foreign to indigenous firms. Skills transfer will most commonly be provided, at least initially, through some form of commercial presence or establishment-related trade. The admission of foreign-based service providers is thus not inconsistent with a process of learning-by-doing. Specific cases of technology transfer in insurance, construction and engineering services and international accounting, referred to in Section B, underline the benefits of skills transfer in a framework of accountability (associated with the operations of multinational enterprises) rather than on the open market. The studies also suggest that a constraint on the transfer of skills may be less a reluctance to impart such skills than limited short-run capacity of recipient countries to absorb and apply the skills offered. In its work in this area the United Nations Centre on Transnational Corporations has found extensive transfers of "soft" technology (management, technical, professional and other skills) and concludes that, in contrast to the situation of manufacturing companies, the skills required for the production of services do not tend to be centralised in parent companies, but rather seem to be spread to host-country operations. Service firms cannot split the production activities of their affiliate networks to the extent their manufacturing counterparts do, to match the factor proportions of sub-processes with the factor prices of host countries (3).

A difficult question arising in respect of skills transfer is whether it may be necessary and feasible to go beyond the present situation in which these transfers are occurring, largely under private sector initiative, and cover them in some way as part of the governmental obligations entered into under the process of multilateral trade liberalisation. While this question goes beyond the scope of this paper it will be touched on briefly in the following sub-section.

Finally, in addition to potential liberalisation gains reflecting factors specific to the service sector it might be expected that there would be benefits of a more general nature; macroeconomic policy is more difficult to implement when a large part of the domestic economy expects to be shielded from the competitive discipline of product and labour markets. Service sector liberalisation might thus increase pressure for lower domestic barriers to the import of goods while reducing the rent-seeking activity associated with protected markets.

iii) The Benefits of Multilateral Action

As exporters, or potential exporters, of services, a number of developing countries will stand to gain tangible benefits from a multilateral process of trade liberalisation. The nature of such gains will depend on the extent to which the multilateral framework facilitates concerted international action to reduce trade barriers to those services in which these LDCs have a particular interest. This in turn will depend largely, though not exclusively, on the treatment within the framework and the negotiating process itself of labour-intensive services or those requiring extensive temporary provider-relocation.

For those LDCs without major, or immediate, export opportunities somewhat different considerations apply. For these countries, liberalisation gains are likely to result more from development opportunities associated with reduced local protection against imports. The question then arises -- why should these benefits not be derived unilaterally rather than in a multilateral framework which might limit developing countries' room to manoeuvre and create obligations which they could otherwise avoid? The answer to this question rests on two contentions.

-- First, in practical terms, the alternative to multilateral liberalisation is likely to be not unilateral relaxation but rather a process of bilateral confrontation. A multilateral process of liberalisation which is rules-based is likely to serve the interests of smaller or more vulnerable members of the international trading community more equitably than will accommodation to bilateral pressure. Illustrations of such pressure are evident in the sectoral experience described in Section B: in insurance with the partial opening of the Republic of Korea's market to US insurers in response to Section 301 investigations and in maritime transport with the anti-dumping enquiry conducted by the European Commission against Hyundai Merchant Marine (of the Republic of Korea) and the investigation of Taiwan's shipping practices by the US Federal Maritime Commission. Without prejudice to the circumstances of these particular cases, and acknowledging that a multilateral approach would in itself be unlikely to remove the prospect of anti-dumping action, developing countries are likely nevertheless to be better off pursuing their interests in a multilateral framework.

-- Second, participation in a multilateral negotiating process will enable developing countries to draw attention to the basic infrastructural disabilities which, for many of them, inhibit the development of their services capacity. The outcome will again depend on the negotiating process itself and opinions are divided on the scope for action but there may nevertheless be opportunities for examination of the role and nature of skills transfers in the liberalisation process as well as recognition of the parallel but distinct question of financial and technical assistance for poorer LDCs.

Beyond this, mention should be made of two additional, related arguments for a multilateral approach. First, developing (and developed) country administrations may find a more receptive domestic response to the removal of local restrictions on service imports in circumstances where other countries are also seen to be making "concessions". Second, an environment of wideranging multilateral discussion covering a large number of sectors may provide an opportunity for participating countries to better assess overall national priorities both as between different service sectors as well as between the interests of service producers and service consumers.

2. The Adjustment Process

As developing country service markets are opened up to external competition there may be a difficult adjustment process. As noted in Section B, and as developed more fully in Part II, adjustment considerations may reflect the particular characteristics of the service in question. These are seen to range over concerns in banking and financial services about access to the financial market by small enterprises; in insurance, arising from the strategic role of insurance companies as financial intermediaries, investing large sums in the economy; and in information, computer and communications services, related to a perceived dependency and vulnerability associated with the storage overseas of sensitive national data bases. Each of these concerns is associated with increased imports of services as trade is liberalised. In tourism and travel there may be additional concerns, related to exports, as increased tourist inflows place pressures on the environment or endanger cultural integrity.

Beyond these sectoral specificities there are, as noted earlier, two aspects of the process of adjustment to a more liberal environment which are relevant to all service activities: possible balance of payments strains, at the macroeconomic level, and, at the microeconomic level, the impact on local producers. These considerations are not, of course, unique to services -- they apply equally to goods trade. However, the complexity of forms through which services can be provided internationally raises considerations specific to service activities.

The most common safeguard reference in sectoral studies of services trade liberalisation relates to balance of payments constraints. Here, however, three distinct aspects need to be distinguished, where:

-- A general balance of payments constraint is invoked in support of import restrictions, including on some services.

-- Persisting balance of payments strains arising from the import of a particular service are invoked in support of import substitution and domestic production of that service.

-- Foreign exchange outflows arising from the import of a particular service, and giving rise to short-term balance of payments strains, are invoked in support of temporary foreign exchange restrictions.

The first of these situations, which relates to resort to GATT Article XVIII:B, is not specific to services trade and will not be pursued here. The second situation reflects widespread developing country concern in a number of sectors, notably insurance, maritime transport and construction and engineering services. A process of services liberalisation may indeed entail an increased and sustained foreign exchange outflow, possibly necessitating import contraction elsewhere, overall demand restraint or exchange rate adjustment. But this will not necessarily be the case. Where liberalisation is achieved through relaxation of conditions relating to commercial presence, although there are likely to be outflows related to dividends or other remittances, there may be no additional balance of payments strain. For example, increased reliance on locally established foreign direct insurers may diminish reliance on international reinsurance and actually reduce foreign exchange outlays. In the construction and engineering sector foreign exchange savings may be realised through resort to the "build, operate, transfer" formula under which the responsibility for project finance rests with the foreign contractor. Moreoever, even where services liberalisation is expected to lead to a sustained increase in imports, the balance of payments argument cannot be invoked in support of import replacement in any particular sector without consideration of alternative areas of import saving and the relative costs of domestic production in each of the activities considered.

The third element outlined above concerns the introduction of temporary restrictions on foreign exchange outflows to cope with demonstrable balance of payments strains resulting from services trade liberalisation. Where such restrictions are specific to a particular service activity and in conformity with any necessary consultation processes they are likely to be regarded as a legitimate form of safeguard action. Such measures are found to be a common developing country practice in tourism and travel, ICC services and professional services. In the banking sector somewhat special considerations may apply. Here any safeguard measures may need to apply only to the capital movements associated with banking and financial services and not to the payments for the services themselves. Where temporary restrictions on foreign exchange outflows relate to the remittance of payments to a foreign-based service provider it will be important that they are not used to limit or frustrate the relationship of the local entity with its foreign parent.

A liberalisation process is also likely to impose strains at the level of the firm, placing local service providers under increased competitive pressure and possibly challenging their market position. Again, however, this will not always be the case -- developing country experience suggests, for example, that in those cases where increased foreign banking presence concentrates on new areas of wholesale banking there may be only limited impact on local banks' traditional retail business. The net employment effect of liberalisation is correspondingly difficult to determine. Where liberalisation relates to cross-border trade there may be employment losses in the local service sector concerned. But these have to be offset against any employment gains resulting from improved export opportunities and from improved efficiency of resource allocation, as well as any possible dynamic efficiency gains. Moreover, where liberalisation relates to establishment-based trade there may be no first-round employment loss in the local industry. Where developing country administrations consider, nevertheless, that it is necessary to assist local service providers in the face of foreign competition care will be needed that such support does not compromise the realisation of potential liberalisation gains. Opportunities might therefore be taken to promote measures which are:

-- time bound, in order not to discourage necessary innovation and flexibility;

-- neutral as between production for the domestic market and for export by focussing less on import restrictions (which may foster domestic sales but tax exports) and more on subsidised support for necessary services infrastructure (which yields comparable benefits to both domestic market and export activity). Somewhat paradoxically -- given the overall case for policy neutrality and non-discrimination between broad industry groups -- where specific support for individual service sectors is considered warranted it is likely that such support will be more effective if applied selectively, it having been suggested that infant industry support is unlikely to succeed if applied to a large number of different activities within any one economy (4). Against this, however, should be set the risks of a "picking winners" approach when based on a possibly unfounded assumption that public authorities have better information on market prospects than is available to private business.

Constraints arising from the balance of payments or from the interests of local service providers should not be invoked against exploring liberalisation opportunities. Nevertheless, they are legitimate concerns which, together with the sector-specific concerns referred to earlier, should be given due weight in the application of a liberalisation process. They underline the need for an approach to liberalisation which is progressive (allowing trade to expand gradually), which encourages forms of trade that facilitate the transfer of skills necessary for the development process and which fosters cooperation with foreign-based service providers in maximising viable opportunities for using local inputs and meeting local user needs (5). Moreover, as seen in Section B, experience in banking and financial services suggests that if overall welfare gains are to be realised, liberalisation measures may need to be accompanied by broad macroeconomic adjustment and be carefully sequenced as between different sectors of the economy.

Finally, it should be acknowledged that in adjusting to a more liberal environment participating countries (developing and developed) will not be required to abandon all of their regulations. Indeed, experience suggests that liberalisation through the removal of discrimination against foreign service providers, whether in banking, in telecommunications network-based services or in other sectors, may in fact require some strengthening of particular regulations where prudential controls or consumer interests are at stake. While liberalisation and de-regulation are often closely linked they are not same.

3. Developing Country Diversity: Prospects for Gain

Section B of this note includes reference to some 46 developing countries whose experience, in varying degrees, bears upon the scope for potential export or development-related gains. The countries, which are referred to for purely illustrative purposes, defy common classification. They range over low-income countries (China, Guinea, India, Kenya, Nepal, Pakistan and Sri Lanka) and upper middle-income economies (Argentina, Brazil, Malaysia, Mexico, and Venezuela), as well as the Newly Industrialising Economies (Hong Kong, Republic of Korea, Singapore and Taiwan). Among the middle-income economies referred to there are those with a strong manufacturing base (such as the Philippines and Thailand) as well as others whose manufacturing sector accounts for only a relatively small share of GDP (such as Indonesia and Nigeria).

However, while the opportunity for gain from liberalisation of trade in services appears to be open to a diverse range of developing countries, this very diversity makes it difficult to establish for any individual country what the nature and extent of net gains might be. This can be seen more explicitly with reference to two particular sectors -- tourism and ICC services.

-- The likely outcome for individual LDCs of liberalised trade in tourism will depend on a complex set of factors, including the capacity to absorb increased tourist flows and to provide intermediate inputs to tourism; the stage of development of the domestic tourism industry; the overall balance of payments situation and vulnerability to import leakage (6); and the growth of disposable income and likely demand for tourism imports (as nationals seek to travel overseas). It might be tentatively suggested that a relatively advanced developing country with extensive restrictions on tourism trade (through constraints on the operation of foreign-based tourism enterprises), but with untapped tourism potential and capacity to provide intermediate inputs efficiently will stand to gain relatively more from trade expansion than will a small island economy with limited economic resources and an already liberal policy environment.

-- In ICC services a distinction can be made (drawing on UNCTC analysis) between the possible policy responses of LDCs at markedly different stages of development. For an advanced developing country with a developed technological and educational infrastructure there may be scope for developing ICC services for the world market, in a framework of trade expansion, and for some measure of infant industry-type support. For those LDCs without the necessary technological and educational back-up but with a potentially large domestic market for ICC services, initial emphasis might be put on infrasturcture development, through joint venture arrangements or other opportunities for skills and technology transfer. Finally, for those LDCs with neither infrastructure support nor significant domestic market potential, the immediate priority is likely to be improved access to information services traded internationally.

While it is necessary to differentiate LDC experience it is also important not to lose sight of broad principles commonly applicable. The distinctions suggested above in respect of ICC services are subject to four qualifications, each of cross-sectoral significance. First, for all developing countries, regardless of their stage of development, there is likely to be scope for development gains by encouraging those forms of trade which facilitate the transfer of skills and soft technology. Second, all countries will gain by encouraging a continuous upgrading of infrastructure development. Third, even poorly endowed developing countries, without major infrastructural support, may be able to develop a market niche at the appropriate level of skill-intensity. Finally, any consideration of infant industry support will need to take careful account of the potential costs and constraints frequently associated with such support.

In short, developing countries need not regard the liberalisation of trade in services as a "negative sum game". There may be only a limited number of LDCs that will gain both extensive export gains across several sectors and widespread development benefits as local protection is reduced. But equally, there are unlikely to be any developing countries that do not have areas of export opportunity that could be better exploited or whose overall resource allocation and development opportunities could not be enhanced by improved access to imported services and the skills transfer with which they are frequently associated.

The outcome for individual developing countries of the liberalisation process is likely to depend on three broad factors:

-- the assessment by each country of its overall priorities, the relative costs of alternative service activities within the economy and the perceived balance of user and provider interests;

-- the willingness of developing country administrations to introduce and sustain liberalisation measures in those areas where reduced import restrictions would create opportunities for development gains; and

-- the ability of the multilateral negotiating framework (7) to help foster LDC export and development gains while allowing adjustment strains to be absorbed gradually.

While it is beyond the scope of this paper to consider these elements in detail, it might nevertheless be suggested, on the basis of the service sectors considered here, that there are likely to be opportunities for developing countries, whatever their circumstances, to gain net benefits from a more liberal, rules-oriented trade environment.

B.   SECTORAL EXPERIENCE

1. Banking and Financial Services

i) Export Opportunities

The potential contribution of trade expansion to the development goals of developing countries will derive, in part, from the increasing, albeit modest, role of some of these countries as the originators of multinational banking operations. While it is widely acknowledged that developed countries have a comparative advantage in the provision of financial services, a measure of developing country competitiveness will reflect the essentially labour-intensive nature of the distribution side of such services, requiring close personal contacts and detailed knowledge of local or regional markets. Bank operating costs in many developing countries are low relative to assets because of low salary scales.

As a reflection of developing countries' revealed comparative advantage, the internationalisation of banking has not been a one-way process (8). In 1978-1979, multinational banking institutions with an LDC country of origin accounted for some 20 per cent of branches and 6 per cent of subsidiaries throughout the world. There is a particularly strong presence of Brazilian and Indian banks. The major banks of these traditional host countries have in turn become multinational and extended their networks in industrialised countries. In 1984, Indian commercial banks had 141 branches operating in 25 countries. International operations which were earlier confined to financing India's foreign trade have now grown to include raising funds in money and capital markets abroad. The active participation of LDCs in international banking is also reflected in the proliferation of offshore centres. Some 20 per cent of euromarket activity is accounted for by LDC offshore centres (in the United Arab Emirates, Bahamas, Cayman Islands, Bahrain, Netherlands Antilles, Panama, Singapore, Philippines and Hong Kong).

ii) Development Gains

It appears that, notwithstanding the growth of foreign banking within developing countries (or perhaps because of it), this growth has been strongly controlled by national authorities and that, overall, restrictions associated with the establishment and operation of foreign institutions in this sector are tighter in developing than in developed countries (9). On the other hand, prudential and supervisory regulations are, typically, less tight.

Where developing country banking sectors are oligopolistic or lacking in competition, the admission of foreign banks can contribute to significant improvement in institutional quality. Liberalisation of trade in banking and financial services, whether cross-border or establishment-based, widens the scope of financial intermediaries' activities enabling them to better exploit economies of scale (10). In most developing countries the range of financial services on offer is quite limited. Domestic sources of long-term funding are very scarce; there may be no interest bearing instrument for parking large volumes of short-term funds; and there may be minimal access to commodity and interest futures markets. Foreign banks can be instrumental in filling such gaps -- as they have been, for example, in Nepal through the provision of term finance. The experience of Brazil and India suggests, in contrasting ways, that legitimate goals of development and the protective environment they can engender may impose a cost in terms of reduced efficiency in the banking and financial sector. In Brazil, infant-industry type protection has produced a banking system which is characterised by one of the highest average industry profit-rates in the Brazilian economy and which could be improved in its ability to promote domestic capital formation. In India, the focus on social banking has seen a remarkable increase in the number of borrowers: from 250 000 to over 22 million in the past 16 years. In contrast to Brazil, India's focus on social needs has led to low profitability of commercial banks. Like Brazil, however, inefficiencies have been identified, including in particular, low direct mobilisation of savings.

Except for retail business, the crucial activity of transforming savings into investment results in financial services that are basically inputs to the production of other goods and services. Forward linkages from banking and financial services are likely to be particularly strong in the case of manufacturing. Input-output data for India and Thailand, for example, show 33 and 43 per cent, respectively, of the banking and financial sector's intermediate services being directed to manufacturing industry. Banking and financial services also play a key role in investment and production decisions in both agriculture (where specialised financial services are of major importance for the realisation of productive potential) and mining (given high levels of capital intensity, frequently with a large foreign exchange component). Policies which increase the price or reduce the availability of banking services are likely to involve important inter-sectoral costs. In particular, such measures are likely to restrict the access of both exporters and importers to the wide range of services that international banks can provide in facilitating international trade; and they may also reduce the scope for inflows of foreign currency frequently associated with foreign banks' activities. A study conducted by the World Bank of 36 countries over 1965-84 supports the proposition that liberalised, market-oriented financial systems promote efficiency and growth.

Perhaps the most significant long-term case for the admission of foreign banks into developing countries is that it facilitates the adaptation of advanced financial sector skills to local conditions. A steady flow of staff at management levels from foreign bank branches to domestic banks is a common occurrence in developing countries. The transfer of skills is likely also to involve an element of complementarity where foreign banks concentrate on their particular areas of expertise (notably trade facilitation and international transfers) rather than on LDC retail banking where their involvement appears to have been relatively modest.

iii) The Adjustment Process

Because of the special characteristics of the banking and financial services sector, banking liberalisation in developing countries may need to take account of three particular considerations, each fully compatible with a process of liberalisation:

-- First, where there is financial distress in the banking sector, the relaxation of restrictions on foreign firms in the absence of more general financial reform and efforts to stabilise the macroeconomic framework may only marginally enhance competition while exacerbating solvency problems in the financial system. The entry of new financial institutions unencumbered with bad portfolios may erode the market position of existing banks (11). Users may benefit from improved services but overall welfare may decline should foreign firms be able to take advantage of protected markets to generate high rents.

-- Second, liberalisation of the financial sector and the capital account if carried out before liberalisation of the current account may, through induced capital inflow, encourage a rapid and destabilising appreciation of the real exchange rate. This appears to have been the experience of Argentina, in contrast to that of Chile where radical reform of trade policy preceded liberalisation of capital account transactions and where the pursuit of outward-oriented policies may have been more effectively sustained (12). (The importance of this consideration will, of course, depend on the finally agreed scope of the liberalisation process and whether capital movements are to be included.)

-- Third, at the microeconomic level, measures may be needed to ensure that a liberalisation process does not inhibit access to the financial market by small enterprises. This is not an insurmountable problem. In the Republic of Korea, as a result of a decision in 1984 to gradually liberalise banking, foreign banks are required to abide by regulations formerly applicable only to domestic banks, including a requirement that 25 per cent of foreign banks' loans must be made to small or medium-sized companies.

As acknowledged earlier these three considerations are not inconsistent with a process of liberalisation. What they underline, however, is the need for LDC liberalisation to be achieved progressively and, in many cases, in conjunction with a broader process of macro-economic adjustment. Moreoever, individual countries in seeking to remove restrictions on trade in financial services will not be required to abandon all of their financial market regulations. Indeed, in some LDCs financial regulations, especially on the prudential side, may need to be made stronger (see Part II, Chapter 1).

2. Insurance

i) Export Opportunities

For most developing countries export opportunities in the insurance sector will be limited. Four particular areas of weakness can be identified -- corresponding closely to those elements on which comparative advantage in insurance is believed to depend (13). Firstly, most new companies in developing countries have unbalanced portfolios. Premium income is unlikely to be high enough to meet liabilities because LDC markets do not produce enough income to allow sufficient spread. Secondly, many local insurance companies in developing countries are likely to be undercapitalised. Thirdly, the technical skills required in insurance will frequently be absent. Finally, most LDC local insurance companies will lack the global diversification associated with the insurance operations of foreign-based insurance companies or the "in-house" insurance companies of transnational enterprises.

Nevertheless, areas of expansion of LDC-based enterprises have been identified through the establishment of subsidiaries in major insurance markets (some twelve UK authorised insurers are from developing countries) and the formation of regional bodies, such as the Arab Reinsurance and Insurance Group which seeks to expand its activities into European and American markets. It has also been observed that an increasing proportion of insurance risk in industrialised countries is being covered by reinsurance from companies in Far-Eastern developing countries, which themselves would be unlikely to be accepted as direct insurers.

ii) Development Gains

Restrictions on international trade in insurance services are widespread in developing countries. Measures cover both cross-border and establishment-based activities and are particularly common in the two areas of insurance that are inherently international -- reinsurance and international transport or cargo insurance. In a survey of insurance developments in developing countries in 1984-1985 (14), it is reported that there is a tendency in several LDCs towards less strict conditions for the admission of new companies or the involvement of the private sector in insurance business. But in several of the countries cited there is no apparent liberalisation in respect of foreign-based insurers (Cameroon, Jamaica, Mexico, Nigeria, Rwanda) while in the remaining countries restrictions on foreign insurers have either been re-affirmed or strengthened (Malaysia, Sri Lanka, United Arab Emirates, Zimbabwe).

While insurance can be a final product it is as an intermediate service that it plays a particularly significant role in developing country economies through: laying-off risks in production and transportation and thus facilitating the flow of goods and services; promoting and channelling savings; and encouraging new technologies, materials and agricultural products, whose vulnerability to loss is uncertain. The costs of inefficiency are correspondingly widespread.

Insurance services in developing countries are frequently more expensive and less efficient than those available in developed countries. The UNCTAD secretariat has noted the probability that services provided by domestic companies in LDCs may not reach the quality level that their economies need, that premium rates are lower in foreign markets and payment of indemnities more generous and prompt (15). Policies that restrict the operation of foreign insurers can thus act as a tax on local buyers of insurance in order to raise the incomes of local sellers. The protective environment engendered by policies of support for local insurers can contribute to inefficiency by inhibiting technology transfer from foreign insurers, fragmenting foreign-based insurers' capital assets through discriminatory deposit or capital requirements, and distorting the portfolios and capital formation process of foreign insurers through requirements for local investment. Distortions may also arise from policies seeking to merge local insurance institutions where the creation of oligopolies may be contrary to consumer interests.

A commonly evoked reason for promoting local insurance capacity in developing countries is the balance of payments strain arising from imported insurance services. This question has been considered, in general terms, in Section A. Two qualifications relate specifically to the insurance industry. First, the outflow resulting from the investment abroad of premiums or reserve funds may over a certain period or under particular circumstances be more than offset by an inflow against claims. Second, reduced reliance on foreign-based direct insurance (as evidenced through widespread indigenisation over the past three decades) is likely to lead to increased dependence on international reinsurance, because of the inability of local insurers to retain the increased business. In such circumstances, any gains through reduced foreign exchange outlays on direct insurance are likely to be significantly eroded. Excessive reliance on reinsurance reduces developing country insurers to little more than brokers, rather than genuine risk carriers, depriving them of income and frustrating their growth. Additionally, undue reliance on international reinsurers, usually without local presence, can expose the countries concerned to the relatively less disciplined insurance environment (in terms of fiduciary regulation and consumer protection) frequently associated with reinsurance.

Significant dependence on international reinsurance will remain as long as underlying economic disabilities persist. Nevertheless, one potential benefit of a trade expansion process might be to help LDCs establish an appropriate balance between domestic and foreign-based insurers such that retention levels were increased (through the admission of branches or subsidiaries of foreign-based insurers) and undue reliance on reinsurance reduced. The alternative policy response of seeking to avoid undue recourse to overseas reinsurance by simply imposing restrictions on it (through compulsory cessions or discriminatory taxation, in the pursuit of self-reliance) fails to address the underlying cause of low retention rates while contributing to distortions to the efficiency of the domestic insurance market. A clear risk with compulsory cessions to local reinsurance companies is that direct insurers may be obliged to pay more for the services they receive than if they were able to deal freely with international reinsurers. Additionally, compulsory cessions may leave the national reinsurer with an unbalanced portfolio obliging it to seek reinsurance elsewhere (16).

Restrictions in the other inherently international area of insurance, cargo insurance, also give rise to significant costs. It is estimated that compulsory local insurance of imports leads to double transport and cargo insurance on some 50 per cent of LDC imports. Commonly, exporters in industrial countries in addition to the policies taken out with the "compulsory insurer" also cover themselves with the domestic insurer known to them (17).

A longer-term benefit from the liberalisation of establishment-based trade will be the dynamic gains from skills transfer. For example, in its operations in Kenya and Nigeria, the American International Group (AIG), while reserving for the home office decisions concerning the structure of the financial portfolio and foreign exchange management, has transferred to local entities 100 per cent of motor vehicle insurance underwriting. In a study of AIG's international operations (18) four forms of technology transfer have been identified: formal training courses covering in-house programmes and financing of employees' training in other institutions; interaction with experts working within the company; knowledge acquired from international telex communication; and the direct transfer of reporting systems, procedures, products and electronic data-processing equipment from the parent company to its subsidiaries. Skills transfer also occurs, more generally, as AIG employees move to other, indigenous, companies. In Nigeria and the Philippines AIG is a substantial net exporter of trained people. The study in question suggests that while certain skills can be learned directly on the open market without giving a multinational firm access to the local direct insurance market, there are nevertheless particular benefits to be derived from skills transfer through continuous, long-term interaction of people within a well-organised framework of accountability.

iii) The Adjustment Process

The process of liberalisation in the insurance sector will raise considerations for developing countries not dissimilar to those in banking and financial services. As evidenced in two widely differing LDC economies, the insurance sector can play a major role in macroeconomic management. The Nigerian insurance market is the largest in Black Africa and fund accumulation has enabled insurance companies to act as financial intermediaries investing large sums in the economy (19). Insurance firms in the Republic of Korea, as de facto saving institutions, are required to purchase government bonds to stabilise the money supply and as institutional investors they may be called upon to help adjust the stock market by reducing or increasing their stock assets.

This strategic role of insurance should not be invoked, however, as an argument against liberalisation but rather as a case for progressive change consistent with overall economic priorities. As with banking, the process of liberalisation need not put prudential control at risk. A distinction might thus be drawn between the prudential requirement (applied on a basis that does not discriminate between local and foreign-based insurers) that a proportion of premiums be retained in the country where risks are covered and any additional requirement for the retention of profits -- those funds not required to cover claims would be liberalised.

The vital place of the insurance industry within LDC economies may indeed argue in favour of multilateral negotiation where the alternative is a process of bilateral accommodation. The partial opening of the insurance market of the Republic of Korea to US insurers in response to Section 301 investigations has led to some apprehensions. It is suggested that, notwithstanding potential efficiency gains, in a situation where the market remains partially cartelised the limited admission of additional firms may create vested interests against a multilateral, rules-oriented approach to liberalisation (20).

3. Tourism and Travel

i) Export Opportunities

Trade in tourism takes place when individuals residing in one country travel to a second country to purchase tourism services or when a purveyor of tourism services resident in one country offers its services in a second country. Developing countries' competitive position in tourism is hard to characterise. The relative factor endowments which many developing countries can draw on (cultural and physical resources, strategic location on international travel paths, relative abundance of low-cost labour) can, and do, provide the basis for an indigenously competitive tourism industry. At the same time, heavy capital requirements and increasingly sophisticated electronic information networks will be beyond the capacity of many LDCs. Competitiveness may also change over time as development progresses. LDC airlines are considered to enter a phase of increasing competitiveness, as lower-wage countries acquire sufficient skills to perform logistical support tasks, followed by diminishing competitiveness, as the rise in the general wage level more than offsets the importance of the skill factor (21). Finally, tourism export opportunities are likely to depend on government support for infrastructure requirements. This is demonstrated by the differing experience among African countries. While Kenya and Tanzania have natural assets which suggest a similar tourism potential, Kenya's greater resource allocation to tourism has led to a much greater rate of relative growth.

A number of developing countries are major participants in international tourism. Mexico, Singapore, Thailand and India are counted among the top 20 income earners in 1985, and multinational hotel chains operate from Colombia, Hong Kong, India and Mexico. But it is the industrialised countries that account for some 80 per cent of tourist "arrivals" and international receipts, and provide the base for the great majority of international tourism enterprises (22).

A process of trade liberalisation might nevertheless be expected to yield significant benefits to LDC tourism exports (23) whether at the level of:

-- the individual traveller, given the large number of countries, predominantly LDC's, that impose restrictions on the amount of currency their citizens may purchase for travel abroad;

23

-- the tourism enterprise, given barriers against the establishment of tourist promotion offices; or

-- the national airline, given that regulation tends to raise the relative traffic-share of high-cost operators.

Freer movement of developing country citizens to work in tourism-related activities overseas might be regarded as a further broad area of potential LDC gain, although not necessarily falling within "tourism", however broadly defined.

ii) Development Gains

Potential gains to developing countries relate to the scope to relax restrictions imposed on the operations of foreign-based tourism enterprises, such as tour operators, travel agents and hotels. Restrictions include controls on access to foreign exchange needed to remit earnings or management fees; excessive local sourcing or employment requirements and restrictions on the import of hotel supplies; minimum local equity requirements; restrictions on the ability of foreign-based enterprises to solicit customers; and preferential treatment of local tourism enterprises through restricted access for foreign firms to reservation systems or local credit sources.

While these measures may reflect legitimate underlying concerns related to economic development and balance of payments constraints they may indeed be counterproductive and will impose a cost by impairing the efficiency of tourism enterprises -- restricting their access to necessary skills and physical inputs and reducing profitability.

To the extent that reduced efficiency causes tourism activity to be lower than it would otherwise be there are likely to be significant inter-sectoral costs reflecting the diverse linkages associated with tourism and travel. While an accurate measurement of the net social gain from tourism is difficult, some measure of the sector's impact can be derived from input-output statistics. Using national input-output data, studies have been conducted for Singapore and Thailand of both the direct and indirect impact of tourism on GDP (24). For Singapore, the value added directly attributable to tourism comprised 2.7 per cent of GDP in 1979 (derived largely in the transport, hotels, retail trade, restaurants, recreation, clothing and electronic goods industries). The indirect effect contributed a further 1.1 per cent. For Thailand, the total impact of tourism on GDP in 1980 was 2.24 per cent. Indirect effects were particularly high (45 per cent of total impact) due to relatively low value-added in the hotel and restaurant industries and the large economic impact of intermediate supplying industries.

In some developing countries, the link between tourism and the agricultural sector can be particularly important and complex. There is evidence, for example, in the Seychelles that while tourism development has competed with agriculture for scarce resources (with rising land prices diverting financial resources away from farming) tourist consumer demand can provide the basis for the growth and diversificiation of agricultural production.

For most developing countries the skills associated with foreign-based tourism enterprises will be particularly important. Indeed it has been suggested, in respect of tourism development in Africa, that the need for external partners is not primarily financial (few African airlines, for example, have been constrained by an inability to raise external loans); it is rather a question of gaining access to "knowledge, communication and organisation" (25). This need is likely to be particularly marked in respect of the design and selling of package tours, given the need for a comprehensive data base on tourist preferences and a network of retail outlets in the tourists' home countries. In some areas there may be a continuing need for foreign skills and organisation (as with overseas retail outlets). In other areas skills transfer will occur as nationals are trained to gradually replace expatriates. It is estimated that in Barbados and Jamaica, after an initially high dependence on expatriate staff, foreign labour now represents less than 1 per cent of total hotel employees (26).

iii) The Adjustment Process

Liberalisation of imports of tourism services will involve two broad areas of adjustment corresponding, respectively to the movement of individual travellers and the operations of tourism enterprises.

Tourism imports associated with residents' overseas travel are a major preoccupation for many developing countries. While developing countries, overall, have a surplus on tourism trade (and developed countries a deficit), in 1985 some 16 highly differentiated LDCs had tourism deficits and many developing countries are concerned by the absolute size of their tourism debits. For most developing countries tourism deficits result from demand-side rather than supply factors (reflecting the fact that travel is highly income-elastic and that in many developing countries there is a new emerging middle-class that wishes to travel). This is the case, for example, in Malaysia, where the "tourism" deficit is in large measure due to merchandise purchases by residents travelling overseas. The relaxation of residents' overseas travel allowances may thus be likened to a reduction in import quotas. Such a process will, for many developing countries, need to be implemented gradually, with due allowance for the overall balance of payments situation.

The relaxation of controls on remittances and import leakage associated with the operations of foreign-based tourism enterprises may also impinge on foreign exchange considerations. Attitudes towards foreign direct investment may also be at issue. While some tourism activities have relatively little investment -- full or partial ownership only accounts for 18 per cent of rooms in LDC foreign-associated hotels (27) -- the capital requirements of tourism development will ensure a continuing role for foreign direct investment. This role is clearly demonstrated by the experience of Mexico where complex interlinkages between LDC debt, foreign investment and tourism development have produced a situation where some 22 per cent of that country's debt equity swaps have involved foreign investment in tourism (28).

Given the particular nature of tourism and travel, adjustment strains can also be associated with increased exports. These relate essentially to the impact of tourist flows on cultural integrity and the environment -- "externalities", where the market does not reflect and balance the full costs and benefits of activities undertaken. The technology embodied in international hotel companies is frequently based on tourism geared to mass tours and large hotels. While this may not always be compatible with the environmental interests of the host country, international tourism enterprises have a strong long-term interest in recognising any such incompatibility, in reaching satisfactory arrangements with host governments and, wherever possible, in ensuring that tourism activities actually contribute to an upgrading of environmental standards.

4. Maritime Transport

i) Export Opportunities

In considering both export opportunities and potential development gains, it is assumed that there is unlikely to be total market failure in maritime transport. Notwithstanding widespread LDC concern about market organisation in shipping services, it appears that the liner trades market is "contestable" (in that established firms are constrained to maintain competitive prices given the constant threat of market entry of competitors) and that the bulk trades are relatively free of government distortion. Potential liberalisation gains in shipping cannot, however, be seen in isolation from the institutional framework. A significant feature of a certain area of shipping activities is the existence of a formal arrangement (the UN Convention on a Code of Conduct for Liner Conferences) which specifically addresses developing country concerns. This gives rise to questions (which it is not possible to address here) about the nature of any coexistence, at least in the forseeable future, between the UN Convention (to which a significant number of OECD Members are not contracting parties) and whatever negotiating framework might be established for maritime transport in the Uruguay Round.

A principal element of shipping costs is the direct wage bill of crew, where most developing countries, with access to low-cost labour, are relatively well placed. However, any analysis of the contribution of wage costs to LDC comparative advantage is complicated by two factors: first, labour mobility in maritime transport and the employment of developing country seafarers by developed country flag operators; and second, the shortage of skilled personnel in many developing countries (notably in Africa and the Middle-East), necessitating the employment of highly paid foreign officers. Moreover, capital charges assume even greater importance than labour costs -- amounting to some 30 per cent or more of total operating costs. It is against this background that special subsidies, favourable depreciation allowances and tax incentives have become increasingly important. Competitiveness is increasingly associated with the level of financial incentives offered by governments. This observation is consistent with the tentative conclusion reached in a study of revealed comparative advantage in various service sectors. Three developing countries, Brazil, Republic of Korea and Taiwan, are found to have a revealed comparative advantage in maritime transport substantially above the level predicted on the basis of relative factor endowments. It is pointed out, however, that the government of each of these countries provides a significant measure of support to the national fleet, via subsidies, as well as protective cargo regulatory measures (29).

The developing market-economy countries have, overall, increased their share of world tonnage from 8.5 per cent in 1975 to 20 per cent in 1988. However, important qualifications are called for. The LDC share is concentrated among a relatively small number of countries. Apart from the open registry flags, very large fleets (over 4 million grt) are confined to nine developing countries (Brazil, China, Hong Kong, India, Iran, Republic of Korea, Philippines, Singapore and Taiwan). Moreover, the Asian region is the only substantial area of net growth in recent years.

ii) Development Gains

The problem of protectionism in international shipping is not a new one, nor is it confined to any one group of countries. It is suggested, however, that while OECD Member countries have, for the most part, had limited freedom to introduce new direct measures (because of their obligations to observe the concept of free and fair competition under Note 1 of the Code of Liberalisation of Current Invisible Operations), no such constraints apply to developing countries (30). Protective devices have thus been adopted by a large number of developing countries notably through unilateral cargo reservation and restrictions on foreign carriers' ability to invest in facilities such as container terminals or multimodal transport infrastructure. Developing countries sometimes characterise their cargo reservation policies as a defensive response to market distortion resulting from subsidised shipbuilding over-capacity. This argument does not appear to be sustainable. LDC cargo reservation, which is concentrated in liner trades, was well established by the time surplus capacity first appeared in liner shipping around the mid 1980s.

Shipping services, whether indigenous or foreign, have been identified as having a direct bearing on the development process by creating pre-conditions for the expansion of trade based on intensified specialisation. The provision of shipping services will depend importantly on interactions with a wide range of other activities including banking, insurance, information, computer and communications services, brokerage, and handling and storage.

Policies which restrain competition in maritime transport, obliging shippers to use less efficient or higher cost operators, shift the burden for supporting the shipping industry to the shipper, the consumer and ultimately to the economy at large. The growing adoption of unilateral cargo reservation and flag preference measures by developing countries thus raises costs, fosters inefficiency and is likely, in its net effect, to impede rather than encourage development efforts.

-- In the liner trades, it has been estimated that rigid adherence to the UN Convention on a Code of Conduct for Liner Conferences would require substantially greater shipping tonnage (without a corresponding increase in goods shipped) (31);

-- In the bulk trades, OECD Member countries have expressed their conviction that cargo sharing leads to substantial increases in transport costs and has a serious effect on the trading interests of all countries;

-- In respect of open registry shipping, it is suggested that the abolition of flags of convenience (or the transfer of ships to registration in the countries of beneficial ownership) would simply shift activity to a higher cost environment, leading to a signficant reduction in the efficiency of sea transport (32).

In addition to fostering competition, a trade expansion process in maritime transport might also be expected to encourage increased technology transfer; both indirectly, by creating a conducive environment (protectionist policies tending to perpetuate technological obsolescence) and directly, by fostering specific channels for technological upgrading, such as joint ventures. A report by the United Nations Centre on Transnational Corporations on the experience of Guyana, Jamaica and Guinea in bauxite/alumina concluded that the resolution of many problems inhibiting a viable shipping operation was achieved through joint ventures concluded between these countries and a foreign partner (33).

Finally, a less protectionist environment might be expected to yield broad, community-wide benefits through more efficient resource allocation arising from reduced financial support for shipping and shipbuilding activities. This proposition does, however, bear on the question of the relative distorting effects of different approaches to support. To the extent that some measure of government assistance for the national flag is considered warranted, direct carrier subsidy (depending on the nature and scale) is likely to be less distortive than barriers to access through cargo reservation. "Subsidy is limited to the carriers supported; reservation tends to raise the market price charged by all carriers, creating a far larger, albeit hidden, subsidy to the industry as a whole" (34).

For some developing countries the pursuit of equity may override considerations of efficiency and economic viability. Hence expressions of concern that as they work for a "legitimate share in the carriage of their foreign trade [developing countries] are being castigated for not allowing the more efficient vessels of the developed countries to do the job of carrying their cargo" (35). Such a perception may also, in part, explain the shift in focus of the UNCTAD Committee on Shipping in recent years from user towards provider interests. One possible benefit of a multilateral process of liberalisation would be to increase the transparency of the economy-wide costs of such a focus.

iii) The Adjustment Process

Notwithstanding major gains in LDC tonnage shares, almost all developing countries continue to experience a large balance of payments deficit in shipping services. The scale of this deficit does not, in itself, provide an argument against liberalisation but it does underline the potential for shipping payments to contribute to the invisibles deficit and the possible need for any process of adjustment to be undertaken gradually.

As in other sectors, the alternative to multilateral negotiation in maritime transport is likely to be bilateral pressure. This is evident in two recent developments referred to earlier: the investigation of Taiwan's shipping practices by the US Federal Maritime Commission and the anti-dumping enquiry conducted by the European Commission against Hyundai Merchant Marine. In response to the EC Commission's finding that Hyundai MM had enjoyed non-commercial advantages granted by the Government of the Republic of Korea (allowing it to operate lower than normal freight rates which inflicted major injury on Community shipowners) the EC Council has imposed a redressive duty on containerised cargoes carried by the line.

5. Construction and Engineering Services

i) Export opportunities

The competitive strength displayed by a number of LDC exporters of construction and engineering services reflects three factors:

-- Availability of low-cost skilled and semi-skilled labour. The origins of the Republic of Korea's major success in this sector came with the supply of unskilled and semi-skilled labour to construction projects in the Middle-East. More recent experience of the Republic of Korea and of Brazil suggests, however, that low-cost professional staff, rather than manual labour, appears to be the major manpower-cost advantage of contractors from these countries (36).

-- Mastery of "mature" technology, adapted to conditions frequently found in developing countries. An example is Brazil's experience in tropical and arid regions gained in part from government financed infrastructure projects during the 1970s.

-- Close relations with host countries. In addition to specific cases of intra-LDC regional co-operation, benefits may have been derived, for example, by Indian contractors from the significant Indian emigrant populations in Asia and Africa. Close links between some developing countries and centrally planned economies may also provide a basis for trade in construction and engineering services although documentation is scarce.

Three observations concerning LDC competitiveness in this sector need to be made. First, as developing country wage levels rise it may be difficult for them to maintain competitive margins. It is significant that the continued competitiveness of construction companies from the Republic of Korea now depends, in part, on a willingness to draw personnel from other, lower-cost, developing countries. The proportion of Korean nationals working on Korea's overseas projects has fallen from 93 per cent in 1979 to 47 per cent in 1986 (37) as new sources of low-cost labour are being drawn from the Philippines, Thailand, Indonesia, and Pakistan. Notwithstanding this flexibility, the Republic of Korea's share of international construction work fell from 11.2 per cent in 1982 to 2.8 per cent in 1987, in part because of rising wage levels, in part because of declining Middle East demand for infrastructure construction, the traditional Korean market focus. Moreover, while low-cost labour benefits developing countries as exporters in the construction and engineering sector, it also benefits developed country contractors. Foreign labour makes up 70 per cent of Japan's overseas construction activity. Second, government support is likely to be a significant factor in the attainment of a competitive export position. (Korean overseas contractors have benefited from a 50 per cent reduction in corporate income tax, accelerated depreciation allowances and a collective guaranty arrangement from designated banks.) Third, LDC competitiveness is still relatively limited in the more skill-intensive areas of feasibility study and design work.

In 1987, 33 of the top 250 international contractors came from developing countries. They were drawn from the Republic of Korea (11 companies); Singapore (four); India (three); Argentina, Brazil, China, Hong Kong, Taiwan and UAE (each with two); and Cyprus, Kuwait and the Philippines (one). Together these companies accounted for some 7 per cent of exports. In the same year, 17 LDC enterprises were included in the top 200 international design firms. They came from the Republic of Korea (four companies); Brazil (three); India and Taiwan (two); and Egypt, Hong Kong, Israel, Lebanon, Pakistan and Saudi Arabia (one) (38).

To realise their full export potential in construction and engineering services, developing countries will -- in addition to upgrading their skills and technology --be concerned to reduce two constraints: an inability to match the financial packages offered by developed country exporters (Korean firms' ratio of financial costs to total sales is more than double that of equivalent Japanese companies); and obstacles raised by host countries to the admission of foreign personnel. Acknowledgement, within a services framework, of the need for some temporary relocation of essential personnel has particular relevance to construction and engineering services. Developing countries' earlier massive involvement in Middle-East construction projects was largely facilitated by the initial absence of restriction on the employment of foreign workers.

An underlying goal of many developing countries will be to seek to emulate in developed country markets at least some of the success they have realised in intra-developing country trade. A multilateral process of trade liberalisation could help facilitate this goal. Korean firms' market share of the U.S. construction and engineering market in 1985 was 0.4 per cent. As of mid-1987, no Korean firm had received a Japanese construction order or incorporated a subsidiary in Japan.

ii) Development Gains

As users of construction and engineering services developing countries are likely to reserve some projects, such as basic (residential) construction, exclusively for local firms (drawing on support from government subsidies, taxation policy or procurement and tendering procedures). Where projects are open to foreign competition there may be local content or establishment requirements (with minimum local equity), together with restrictions on capital transfers and profit repatriation. Such policies may be applied notwithstanding (or perhaps because of) a frequently observed tendency for clients in developing countries to prefer the services of foreign engineering services firms (39).

Construction and engineering activities within developing countries are often seen as the foundation on which development efforts are established. Backward linkages can have an important impact on relatively unsophisticated labour-intensive domestic industries such as cement and steel manufacturing while forward linkages affect practically all other sectors of the economy. The services associated with construction and engineering occupy an important intersection, drawing together information flows, capital goods manufacture and the financial system. Because of their influence on manpower training and technical and management capacities, consultancy and engineering are seen as having a significant effect on a country's style of development (40).

The experience of India suggests that policies of import substitution can serve to stimulate local technological effort. At the same time, local engineering services firms have been denied ready exposure to imported technology and to the demonstration effects of a more liberal, export-oriented environment. Moreover, due to the lack of innovation in Indian industry, little pressure has been exerted to enhance design capability (41).

As their technological capabilities and expectations expanded in the 1960s and 1970s, many developing countries sought increased technology transfer from overseas contractors. In the process, advanced technology firms are likely to have increasingly acknowledged the net gains (for them) of technology transfer, as a condition for securing business. A principal constraint on technology transfer in construction and engineering services is thus likely to be the capacity of the host country to absorb the imported technology. This is a common theme of three independent case studies in this sector covering, respectively, Colombia; the Republic of Korea, Mexico and Taiwan; and Argentina, Brazil, the Republic of Korea and the Philippines (42). In many developing countries there is a high incidence of recruitment of foreign experts on a short-term basis for the resolution of specific technological problems. It appears, however, that local engineering services firms retain few full-time foreign staff apart from in special cases. The experience of the Bechtel organisation (43) is illustrative of this and of other aspects of technology transfer. The 30-year time span necessary for construction of the Caracas Metro has enabled Bechtel to move from a joint venture participant to that of a partner with a Venezuelan engineering company that is increasingly assuming more responsibility and control. An earlier partnership between Bechtel and the Mexican engineering firm, Ingenieros Civiles Asociados, for the construction of electrical generating facilities, led to the eventual transfer of total responsibility to the Mexican company. In these and other projects, there is a continuous process of training, the objective being to prepare national employees to replace foreign employees in the shortest possible time. To increase the opportunities for technology transfer, Bechtel uses a "components approach" whereby contract packages are tailored to use existing client and national capabilities without jeopardising overall project control.

iii) The Adjustment Process

The process of adjustment to a more liberal environment raises considerations similar to those in other sectors but with elements of specificity. In particular, it would be necessary to:

-- avoid major balance of payments disruption associated with large-scale projects. This may be facilitated by resort, for example, to the "build, operate, transfer" formula whereby the foreign contractor is responsible for financing the project and ensuring its viability;

-- foster a complementary relationship between domestic and foreign construction and engineering services, where a co-operative mechanism between the two facilitates the optimum use of local inputs while fully drawing on foreign resources as a vehicle for the transfer of skills and technology.

6. Professional Services

The diverse nature of professional services together with customary data deficiencies place limits on any general examination of this subject. The field tends to overlap with other sectors which warrant consideration in their own right. Elements of arms-length business co-exist with intra-firm transactions, while trade at the level of the firm occurs side-by-side with the activities of individual practitioners. Moreover, at the level of the individual service provider it is critically important to distinguish the temporary relocation overseas of practitioners whose physical presence is essential for the provision of the service and the longer-term migration of individual practitioners. Such migration will be regarded here as beyond the scope of trade in services.

i) Export opportunities

In exporting professional services developing countries are able to benefit from the availability of relatively low-cost practitioners. (Many professional services are relatively labour-intensive and are thus becoming more expensive in developed countries, while offering only limited opportunities for productivity improvement.) Two other areas of LDC strength apply particularly to the scope for export to other developing countries: familiarity with the particular concerns of developing country consumers of professional services; and close relations with other developing countries, arising either from specific cases of intra-LDC regional co-operation or from cultural or other affinities. However, for all but a relatively small number of developing countries the role of LDCs as exporters of professional services is likely to be limited to the activities of individual practitioners and the members of international teams. At the level of the firm, the international accounting, advertising and legal enterprises based in developed countries are likely to retain a large measure of competitive advantage as they draw on the benefits of economies of scale, ready access to increasingly sophisticated electronic information networks and established links with their multinational enterprise clients. Moreover, international professional service firms are now seeking to replicate their growth in traditional markets by building practices within developing countries.

At the level of the individual practitioner, the experience of Tunisia illustrates the potential scope of export activity (44). In 1986, Tunisia supplied 7 000 professionals throughout French-speaking Africa, the Maghreb and the Middle East, compared with some 1 000 in 1982. An export opportunity has arisen from a domestic surplus of highly educated nationals (ranging over engineers, doctors and qualified security guards) capable of speaking French and Arabic. It is suggested that Tunisian professionals are increasingly replacing European practitioners for one-half to one-third of their cost. It should be acknowledged, however, that some of this outflow may represent permanent migration and as such would not constitute a service "export". In some sub-sectors, developing countries have also succeeded in establishing a presence at the enterprise level. International hospital management or health care companies operate from Bahrain, Brazil, Ecuador, Egypt, Panama, Saudi Arabia, Singapore, Venezuela and the United Arab Emirates.

The ability of developing countries to realise their export potential in professional services will depend, in part, on the scope for foreign consumers to move to the supplier of the service. This will occur, for example, when patients travel overseas to receive medical attention or when students study abroad. The scope for movement here will depend, inter alia, on the availability in the consumer's home country of, respectively, medical insurance for treatment received overseas and funding of education services received in foreign institutions. Perhaps more importantly, however, export growth is likely to depend on wider recognition that the temporary movement of practitioners is necessary for the performance of the service in question. Given the nature of the relative competitive strengths of developed and developing countries in professional services, the issues raised may, in part, mirror the labour/capital focus of the broader debate about factor mobility. Developing countries are thus, overall, more likely to be concerned about barriers to the temporary movement of individual practitioners than they are about establishment-type impediments to professional services at the level of the firm (notably in accounting and advertising). What this means, however, is that the focus of LDC concerns would lead directly into some of the more intractable problems associated with trade in professional services, in particular, certification procedures and mutual recognition of qualifications.

ii) Development Gains

At the level of the firm (and with particular focus on accounting and advertising) impediments to trade appear to be more widespread in developing than in developed countries, although regulations aimed specifically at consumer protection may be more common in developed countries. At the level of the individual practitioner, such a broad assessment of incidence is not possible; it appears, however, that the professions continue to be highly regulated in all countries (45). Regulations are likely to affect the right to practice, the scope of activity and use of firm name. Two areas have been identified as causing particularly serious impediments to trade: restrictions on the repatriation of fees, royalties and profits and restricted access (or the prospect of restricted access) to information and telecommunications services. As the international activity of the professions becomes increasingly dependent on access to data bases and telecommunications networks, restrictions on transborder data flows, on access to private leased line capacity, and on the use of computer facilities in foreign countries are likely to become of growing importance as impediments to the effective transmission of professional services (46).

Professional activities are likely to have strong, specific linkages to other sectors. In directing their clients towards accounting services, banks are likely to choose those firms with which they have ownership or other close associations; advertising activities have important linkages with market research and strategic planning, as well as with the video/TV/media industry. At the governmental level, it is suggested that international accounting firms play a major role as independent advisors to the public sector; contributing to improved financial management, better revenue collection systems and more effective management of government agencies and public enterprises (47).

Restrictions on trade in professional services, whether at the level of the firm or the individual, serve to inhibit innovation and increase costs to the economy as a whole, while placing foreign professional service firms at a competitive disadvantage relative to domestic firms. Given the linkages between professional services and other areas of economic activity, inefficiencies in the professions will entail important costs to the rest of the economy. This may be particularly the case where restrictive practices in the professions, such as collective fee setting and entry or advertising restrictions, raise the price or limit the provision of the service offered. Among the most costly impediments will be those that restrict transborder data flows and access to information, computer and communications services.

Denying market access and associated market presence to international professional service firms that have particular expertise in serving multinational customers is likely to be counterproductive where this simply prompts the multinationals concerned to bypass local restrictions and purchase the needed expertise abroad. Opportunities will be forgone for the expansion of local employment and production and the fostering of local expertise (48).

In the accountancy field, for example, the scope for the transfer of skills is illustrated by the operating practice of international accountants, Arthur Andersen & Co. (49). As new practices are established, ownership and management responsibility is continually turned over to nationals of the country concerned. The resulting affiliated national firms, or "national practice entities", gain skills transfer through the temporary assignment of expatriates and through access to worldwide training, professional education programmes and technical information provided by the international organisation.

iii) The Adjustment Process

The opening up of the provision of professional services in developing countries is likely to involve particular sensitivities.

-- Some professional services (notably advertising and the performing arts) are likely to be susceptible to regulation on the grounds of preserving the cultural integrity of the host nation. While legitimate concerns and moral values will not be put in question, care will be needed that such concerns are not used as a pretext for protectionist policies and that opportunities are taken to develop local participation and strengthen local capacities as an alternative to outright restrictions on imported services.

-- Questions of cultural integrity are likely to be closely related to those impinging on national security and sovereignty. The range of such concerns can be quite broad. Controls on transborder data flows have been motivated, in part, by security-related concerns that, for example, certain data bases be stored domestically. Complex questions may also arise when foreign lawyers are employed to defend the interests of multinational enterprises engaged in legal action against host developing country (or indeed developed country) governments.

Adjustment to trade expansion in professional services can, as with Tourism, entail strains resulting from increased exports. As in Tourism, "public goods" are involved, in this case the cost of the outflow of skilled human resources. In some situations the temporary outflow may provide a safety valve for unemployed professionals - people who, in any event, are likely to retain ethnic ties to the sending country (50). But in other cases significant costs may be entailed. While the nature of such costs cannot be explored here it can be noted, again, that the strains of adjustment will be more readily accommodated in a gradual process of liberalisation.

7. Information, Computer and Communications Services

i) Export Opportunities

Developing countries' potential competitive strengths in specific areas of information, computer and communications (ICC) services are likely to reflect two elements: declining entry costs and labour-intensity. Entry may be facilitated as advances in microelectronics reduce the costs of communications and as economies of scale are realised. Once worldwide information networks are established, the incremental costs of additional ICC services may be relatively low. Labour-intensive production is a characteristic of, in particular, three branches of ICC services: data processing, data input and software production. There are nevertheless constraints on the realisation of each of these elements of competitiveness. Costs of entry will be lowered if all that is required is simply to "plug in" to the network. But this will not be the case if an independent information network is required or if basic telecommunications infrastructure is seriously deficient. Opportunities arising from labour-intensity will be qualified where a high level of skill and capital-intensity is also required. Software has to be machine-tested and relatively sophisticated software calls for correspondingly advanced machinery. Moreover, technological change may serve to erode the opportunities for labour-intensive production, as with the generalisation of character recognition by computer (for data input) or with the development of computer-aided software production.

Notwithstanding these limitations, scattered data on developing countries' revealed comparative advantage in ICC services suggests a small but growing role:

-- Developing countries are not yet important producers of on-line data bases, and their role is largely confined to providing information to the major producers. Some LDCs have nevertheless developed an export capacity -- CMA Engenharia de Sistemas of Brazil exports to Argentina, Uruguay and, more recently, has begun exporting to the United States.

-- Among the world's 100 leading data processing companies there is only one LDC enterprise (Samsung of the Republic of Korea, ranked 68th in June 1987). Nevertheless, opportunities exist. The Caribbean has become the centre of the U.S. "offshore office" operations, in a process similar to the offshore processing of goods such as textiles and electronic components. American Airlines operations in Barbados have been "externalised" with a subsidiary being established selling data processing services in the open market.

-- There has been a significant transfer to LDCs of data input requirements of U.S. corporations. The U.S. imports key punching services from the Philippines and the Republic of Korea.

-- Software production activity in developing country markets is growing. Estimates for 1987 suggest that Brazil's domestic software market will be ranked 10th in the world. Brazil's exports are said to be growing rapidly, as are those from India. India's Tata Consultancy numbers American Express, British American Tobacco and Young and Rubicam among its clients. Other countries, such as Singapore, have set up plans to become information technology exporters.

-- Developing countries are becoming increasingly involved in the establishment of high speed <u>telecommunications</u> (teleport) facilities as evidenced by a recent joint venture between the government of Jamaica and companies from the US and Japan, and a proposed agreement between the Indian Ministry of Science and Technology and the Massachusetts Office of International Trade and Investment.

ii) Development Gains

Some 60 countries have adopted some form of official "informatics policy" (51), most of them dealing with the procurement and use of data processing equipment, but also having implications for transborder data flows. As international economic activity becomes rapidly more information-intensive, any barriers to trade in ICC services will be increasingly perceived as an irritant. Increased awareness of barriers may also mean that protectionist tendencies are growing, particularly in the case of developing countries (52), although this is difficult to assess. Infant industry-type support of software and processing services has been identified in a number of developing (and developed) countries, whether through incentives to foreign companies to establish affiliates (Singapore), restrictions on market access and transborder data flows, (Brazil, Mexico, Nigeria, Thailand and the Middle East), establishment limits (Brazil, Malaysia, Mexico, Saudi Arabia) or through discriminatory taxation (the Republic of Korea, Malaysia, Thailand). Under a recent policy package prepared in India, exporters of computer software will receive all the tax benefits presently applicable to other exports.

The merging of computer and communications technologies has produced an area of services activity that is not only important in its own right, but also a vital element in the conduct and trade of all other service activities. The impact, however, extends well beyond the service sector. Among the advanced industrial countries, ICC technologies are expected to be at the root of a new wave of growth, their strategic importance arising, in part, from new networking applications which strengthen links between users, manufacturers and service providers. ICC services can provide a stimulus both at the microeconomic level, in increasing productivity competitiveness, and at the macroeconomic level, in fostering growth and diversification of the economy. Specific backward linkages lead into telecommunications infrastructure and equipment. While input-output data suggest that forward linkages are strongest towards other service sectors, followed by mining and manufacturing and then agriculture (53) this fails to capture fully the qualitative importance of information services in, for example, helping increase the transparency of commodity markets and their efficiency in responding to changing circumstances.

While the "informatics" policies of many developing countries may have contributed to local production capacities and to some specific areas of export opportunity this will have been achieved at a cost.

-- From a _user_ perspective, national policies that impede unnecessarily the movement of information or that require local duplication of information can entail a high cost and be a serious disincentive to trade. The requirement imposed by the Special Secretariat of Informatics (SEI) in 1981 that VARIG, the Brazilian international airline, move its reservation systems from Atlanta, USA to Rio de Janeiro cost the airline $23 million in reinstallation charges. User costs will also have arisen from the fact that the allocation of resources to the communications infrastructure in developing countries has been much less than market signals have called for. In many LDCs, authorities have restricted the flow of financial and human resources into government monopoly telecommunications and inhibited the efficient management of those resources. A clear example of user-disability is presented by the experience of the maquiladoras -- the industrial plants located in Mexico that typically assemble semi-finished products for US firms. It is reported that, although the situation is improving, the telecommunications services provided between Mexico and Texas by Mexico's Secretariat of Communications and Transportation not only have not satisfied the needs of the new border industries, but have represented a major obstacle for the development and operation of new projects in the manufacturing sector (54).

-- Efficiency gains are not restricted to user interests. Some _producers_ of ICC services might be expected to gain from a trade expansion process. Protection granted to one branch of ICC services may, in some circumstances, have harmful repercussions on other branches. For example, policies which hinder the import of software in areas where domestic substitutes are unavailable may adversely affect the local computer industry and the domestic hardware market.

-- Given the central role played by ICC services, any efficiency gains will have a ripple effect _economy-wide_. Trade expansion in ICC services would thus yield significant inter-sectoral benefits. This is the other side of the coin in respect of Brazil's informatics policy. The former director of SEI has asserted that Brazilian industry is uncompetitive, incompatible with the rest of the world and should be opened up (55).

The rapidly evolving nature of many ICC services raises the complex question of intellectual property rights (IPRs) and the need to balance, on the one hand, the fact that creative activity needs to be encouraged and, as necessary, protected and, on the other hand, fears that exclusive IPRs can entail an anti-competitive element. Against this background, a principal benefit of a more outward-oriented approach to ICC policy is likely to be the transfer of skills associated with foreign-based service providers. The risks of technological change overtaking developing countries' competitive strengths in software production can be reduced through the creation of joint ventures and associated technology transfer. In the 18 months to mid-1986, Japanese firms established no less than 12 joint ventures for software development in developing countries (in China, the Republic of Korea and Taiwan). Texas

Instruments recently entered a software joint venture in the Karnataka State of India, contributing $1 million to a satellite ground station. In Latin America, the attitude of Mexico towards joint ventures -- regarding them as a mechanism for the dissemination of new technology -- presents an interesting contrast with the policy adopted in Brazil (56).

iii) The Adjustment Process

Given the sensitivities of many developing countries in the area of ICC services, a process of liberalisation would need to take account of three particular considerations, each going beyond immediate questions of "trade".

-- First, due allowance would need to be made for developments in the institutional environment. It is planned, for example, to begin a review of a number of the Recommendations of the International Telecommunication Union. Any such review would clearly need to take full account of developing country interests and of the need for complementarity with the parallel activities within the GATT. The issue of reforming Intelsat and addressing its pricing and marketing policies is also closely tied with the question of meeting developing country concerns. Intelsat's price structure is based on international geographic route averaging which benefits thin traffic regions, that is, mainly developing country regions. Such benefits would be at risk in the event of a liberal international convention which led to private company networks carrying third party traffic, thus diverting traffic from Intelsat.

-- Second, consideration would need to be given to a recurring developing country concern related to dependence and a consequent perception of vulnerability. This concern may arise from specific access-to-data questions associated with the storage overseas of nationally important data bases. It may also arise from more general fears that ICC services provide the basis for the centralisation of corporate decision-making, marginalising the role of multinational enterprises' LDC affiliates (notwithstanding the fact that MNE centralisation policies of the 1970s appear to have given way to a more flexible approach based on corporate preferences and country characteristics).

-- Third, there would need to be recognition of the fact that while certain forms of services trade may assist the development process, a purely trade-oriented approach would not address the underlying problems faced by those LDCs with inadequate ICC infrastructure. The scope for these countries to take full advantage of potential liberalisation gains will depend, in part, on parallel development assistance efforts to improve their educational and technical resources. Recent discussion in OECD has identified an increasing infrastructural and technological gap in communications and related sectors between developed and developing countries which "will affect international patterns of investment and trade for decades to come" (57).

1. Banking and Financial Services

a. Introduction

The internationalisation of banking and financial services has important implications for developing countries, both as hosts and originators of multinational banking operations. In the process of internationalisation there has been a tendency, in a wide range of countries (developed and developing), for elements of liberalisation of cross-border financial flows, the entry of foreign financial institutions and domestic financial market deregulation to be combined with the maintenance or even tightening of certain regulatory controls, whether for reasons of prudential supervision, monetary policy, economic development or infant industry support. In large measure, this reflects the fact that the provision of banking and financial services is closely interlinked with fundamental questions relating to the international credit situation, exchange rate management and domestic monetary targeting. A distinction will be drawn here between liberalisation of trade in financial services and deregulation of financial markets. While these concepts tend to go hand in hand in the sense that progress in one creates strong pressures for movement in the other, they are not the same. Individual countries in seeking to remove discriminatory restrictions on trade in financial services will not be required to abandon all of their financial market regulations. Indeed in some countries financial regulations, especially on the prudential side, may need to be made stronger.

The development of more efficient financial markets, in mobilising savings and channelling those savings (together with capital from the international financial markets) to productive investment, is a critical need in most developing countries. A question which may arise for many of these countries is the extent to which both cross-border and establishment-based trade in financial services would contribute to such development.

It appears that in many developing countries there are clear opportunities for complementarity between domestic and foreign banks, where the latter concentrate on the trade and investment facilitation aspects of banking and financial services or, more generally, wholesale banking activities in which they have particular expertise.

b. Sector Profile

A broad approach to banking and financial services will be adopted, covering a wide range of activities: retail banking (deposit taking, lending, advisory services, etc.); corporate financial services (financial management, capital raising, etc.); securities-related financial services; inter-bank services (money-market transactions, clearing and settlement, etc.); and international financial services (import and export financing, foreign exchange trading, etc.) Banking and financial services are thus made up of a large number of sub-sectors. For developing countries, as a whole, the relative importance of these sub-sectors is likely to differ from that in developed countries and, for the most part, the focus here will be on traditional banking services. Consideration will be given to both banking activities in developing countries and with developing countries. Trade in banking and financial services will thus be taken to include both business conducted through foreign establishment and through cross-border operations.

Banking and financial services have witnessed intensified competition in recent years. The rapid evolution of the industry has contained a number of important elements: financial innovation, including securitisation and the growth of financial intermediation outside the banking system; deregulation of national financial markets, including growth of new entrants and increased authority for financial institutions to carry out a broader range of activities, tempered however by a growing concern for harmonised standards of prudential supervision; and rapid growth of information technology, an important complement to diversification and innovation in financial services. A further element, and one which has perhaps impacted most immediately on developing countries, is the internationalisation of banking and financial services, a process which has been facilitated by a progressive liberalisation of exchange controls. Three underlying forces have been identified (58):

-- The initial impetus, from the early 1960s, came from the expansion abroad of non-financial corporations and the demand for domestic banks to follow their customers.

-- By the late 1960s the rapid growth of international wholesale banking, particularly in the eurocurrency markets, provided an additional incentive for banks to move to the major financial centres and in some cases to developing countries that were becoming increasingly significant borrowers from international banks.

-- A third force of expansion, in the mid 1970s, reflected banks' realisation that the growing interpenetration of national economies and financial markets made physical presence in foreign countries a prerequisite for maintaining market shares.

Looking ahead, foreign banks are likely to continue to be mainly interested in corporate or wholesale banking -- in doing business with larger companies, both foreign and domestic, mainly for trade financing purposes and project financing. At the same time, the third of the elements outlined above could assume increasing importance as a sharp drop in direct investment in developing countries and increased use by multinational enterprises of forms of investment requiring a reduced commitment of equity capital is lessening the need for customer-following, and as LDC debt constraints and changes in the oil market situation impact on banks' international financial activities. Given the sensitivities associated with retail banking in many host developing countries, this would have important implications for the process of liberalisation of trade in financial services.

The nature of foreign banking in developing countries in recent years has also been affected by the switch in interest in development finance from credit to other forms of finance providing equity or equity-related services (59). As banks and other financial institutions seek to convert problem debt into equity, venture banking (where banks provide equity investment) may assume growing importance. This will have implications not only for cross-border investment directly to the end user, but also for investment in subsidiary or joint venture activities of banks and other financial institutions themselves.

Based on case studies of eleven developing countries (60), the establishment of foreign banks in developing countries appears to have intensified from the mid 1970s. This is particularly marked in Argentina, Egypt, Ivory Coast, Republic of Korea, Philippines and Singapore. In the areas of deposit taking and extension of credits the extent of foreign bank activity in local business shows considerable inter-country diversity (with high levels in the Ivory Coast, Lebanon and Singapore, which are regional financial markets, and relatively modest shares in the remaining countries -- see Table 1). Levels of activity are uniformly high however in the traditional areas of operation of foreign banks -- foreign exchange, international transfers and export credits. In all the countries of the sample, the vast majority of clients of foreign banks is made up of foreign multinational firms and major local firms. As a general rule, the foreign banks have shown very limited involvement with households, small and medium-sized business and with the rural sector.

Table 1

FOREIGN BANKS SHARE IN LOCAL DEPOSITS AND CREDITS
1979-1980

Country	Percentage total advances	Percentage total deposits
Argentina	11	12
Brazil	13.8	9.25
Korea	9.2	1.4
Ivory Coast	-	75
Egypt	11.4	18
India	4	3.4
Lebanon	42.8	47.6
Mexico	-	-
Peru	2.4	3.4
Philippines	13.4	-
Singapore	64 (1)	54 (2)

1.   Of which 3.5 per cent with offshore banks.
2.   Of which 1 per cent by offshore banks.

Source: Germidis et al, International Banks and Financial Markets in Developing Countries.

As indicated in Part IB the internationalisation of banking has not been a one-way process -- developing country banks have a significant overseas presence.

Some developing countries (such as Singapore in the 1970s) have encouraged financial services for their own intrinsic contribution to economic activity or to lessen dependence on manufacturing. More commonly, however, banking and financial services are likely to be seen in a broader context. The sector is central to monetary policy and overall economic management -- playing a role that cannot be measured simply in terms of its own immediate output. The importance to economic development of a stable and efficient financial system for collecting savings and channeling funds to productive investments is evident. Whether "demand following" or "supply leading" the sector is clearly inextricably linked to the development process.

c. Developing Country Concerns

Four groups of concerns have been identified. They relate to prudential supervision, monetary policy, economic development and infant industry type considerations and are listed with a progressively increasing, but not exclusive, developing country focus. Where appropriate, the nature of these concerns will be illustrated by associated policy measures adopted in particular developing countries. The dividing line between different developing country concerns with respect to trade in financial services is not always clear; there is no simple, one-to-one relationship between concerns and measures; single policy instruments are frequently applied in response to a number of underlying concerns. Moreover, policy instruments will relate to both cross-border and establishment-based trade -- with differing implications for the relative treatment of domestic and foreign banks. Where, for example, a country is concerned about the independence of its monetary policy, it may seek to maintain that independence with exchange controls (impinging on cross-border financial services). Domestic and foreign-owned established banks can equally be subjected to such controls. Developing countries may also argue, however, that foreign banks have a greater capability to evade monetary policy-related regulations and may thus seek to limit the presence of foreign banks or to treat foreign-established banks in a discriminatory manner.

Banking and financial services are quite closely regulated in all countries and the concerns which prompt these regulations are not exclusive to developing countries. Nevertheless, as noted earlier it appears that, overall, restrictions or conditions associated with the establishment and operation of foreign institutions in the banking and financial services sector are tighter in developing than in developed countries. (On the other hand, prudential and supervisory regulations are, typically, less well developed). In a study of entry restrictions facing United States banks there were seen to be relatively few cases of a total absence of foreign bank presence (12 countries, of which eight were LDCs and four were centrally planned economies, CPE) or of total exclusion of new bank entry (19 developing or CPE countries). There were, however, widespread cases where foreign commercial bank branches were restricted (76 countries of which 66 were LDC or CPE) or where equity interest in indigenous commercial banks was prohibited (56 countries of which 50 were LDC or CPE) (61).

43

i) Prudential supervision

Prudential supervision is motivated both by a desire to protect the consumer and by concern about the effects of any serious bank failure on the economy and on public confidence in the financial system. Reliance on market discipline is unlikely to provide sufficient reassurance, given the high social costs of the ultimate market discipline -- bank failure. Supervisory authorities have thus acquired greater responsibilities in recent years, particularly in ensuring that banks' control systems are adapted to the requirements of more sophisticated and active markets (62). Supervisory control can be seen to have increased significantly in two markedly different developing country economies.

-- In Hong Kong, following a series of bank collapses over the preceding three years (one of which involving the Hong Kong Bank costing an estimated HK$ 1 billion), a new regulatory regime was introduced in September 1986. The new regulations involve requirements on capital adequacy; Government approval for all new shareholdings representing more than 10 per cent of a bank's equity; and a requirement to cede control if the Banking Commissioner deems this necessary in the public interest.

-- The Government of Malaysia, in late 1985, moved to ease strains on the banking and financial sector, resulting from deep-seated economic problems linked to depressed commodity prices. The new measures involve restrictions on future bank ownership to 20 per cent for a corporation and 10 per cent for an individual or family; and authority for the Central Bank to take over a financially troubled bank or finance company. It is significant, however, that these measures of prudential control were accompanied by liberalising action elsewhere (as in permitting banks to take up majority stakes in local stockbroking companies) as part of the Government's commitment to deregulation. This case illustrates the importance of distinguishing, wherever practicable, between prudential and supervisory regulations on the one hand, and other types of financial market regulation that have the objective in effect of limiting competition, on the other. Financial market deregulation often has to be flanked with a strengthening of prudential controls.

A question arising is the extent to which measures of prudential supervision serve to discriminate against foreign-owned financial institutions. In Pakistan, for example, it is understood that, at the time of writing, foreign banks must maintain a minimum capital of 5 million rupees or 7.5 per cent of their total deposits, whichever is higher. The corresponding levels for nationalised banks are 2 million rupees or 5 per cent of deposits. It has been observed that even well-intentioned Governments will find it hard to apply capital adequacy requirements in ways that do not incidentally discriminate against foreign banks. It is thus suggested that to require that a foreign bank show evidence of its assets and, at the same time, to allow it to use its foreign-held assets to meet solvency requirements, exposes host countries to the danger that if the same assets are used to guarantee the solvency of several independent operations, they may be inadequate as cover against the independent risks to which the multinational bank, as a whole, is subject. Where "appropriate" regulations are identified (whether in developing or developed countries) it will be important to acknowledge that, liberalisation notwithstanding, some degree of regulatory control may need to subsist. Two critical issues thus emerge: first, the avoidance of regulations that are more onerous than underlying concerns warrant and, second, the avoidance of discrimination where alternative nondiscriminatory but still effective approaches are available. These are not easy issues to address. As far as possible, it will be necessary to differentiate between branches and subsidiaries. The latter should be treated in the same way as domestic banks. Branches raise more difficult considerations but the objective might be "equivalent treatment", taking into account the difficulty of comparing foreign branches with domestic banks. On those limited occasions when valid prudential concerns justify discriminatory regulations the burden should be on those imposing such regulations to demonstrate the need for discrimination.

ii) Monetary policy and macro-economic management

Concerns about prudential supervision are closely related to those associated with macro-economic management. In the latter case, however, restrictions are more likely to be openly discriminatory. Banking, because of its close links with a country's monetary policy, is frequently seen as raising questions of dependency and hence national sovereignty, leading into a more general, political concern about foreign control of important or sensitive sectors.

More specifically, some would claim that foreign financial institutions, by their very "foreignness" can compromise domestic policy measures. They may be tempted to evade domestic taxes or exchange controls by off-market pricing of inter-bank foreign exchange transactions, by "parking" funds in tax havens or by "round tripping" to avoid restrictive monetary policies (63). In view of their wider range of opportunities international banks' branches in any particular country are indeed likely to be less bound by the constraints of that country's monetary policy than are domestic banks. They are better able to take advantage of differences in interest rates and are never entirely dependent on the local market for resources -- being able to call upon other branches of the bank and particularly on those located in international financial centres. In practical terms, drawing on the case studies referred to earlier, the experience of developing countries in intrabank international financing is seen to vary considerably.

-- In the Philippines, the Republic of Korea and Brazil the end result of foreign banks using their capacity to finance themselves from other branches within their groups is an inflow of foreign currencies into the economy. The situation is different, however, in Singapore, where foreign banks turn to the interbank market, dominated by domestic banks, and in the Ivory Coast, where foreign banks are refinanced with the Central Bank. In **Argentina**, **Peru** and **India** foreign banks' deposits and credits are broadly in balance and neither interbank nor intrabank resources are much resorted to.

Concerns about the independence of monetary policy and fears about the capability of foreign banks to evade such policy are thus an important contributor to the widespread controls on the establishment of foreign banks. In addition, monetary policy considerations will contribute to controls on the operations of foreign banks. These may take the form, for example, of restrictions on local currency/foreign currency swap agreements. In moves aimed at reducing the growth of money supply, the Bank of **Korea** recently allowed foreign banks to issue certificates of deposit for the first time, but on the basis that the amount of foreign exchange they can swap for Korean won will be reduced automatically by the amount of CDs issued. Foreign banks in the Republic of Korea usually obtain won for domestic lending by selling a portion of their foreign currency brought from their head offices under an agreement with the Bank of Korea.

While the close relationship of foreign banks to the international market is one of their strengths, this relationship may create concerns about circumvention of domestic monetary policy. The most important set of controls with a monetary policy justification relate to cross-border trade in financial services and the effectiveness of exchange controls. While such controls are applied to domestic banks as well as to established foreign-owned banks, exchange controls affecting capital movements and foreign exchange transactions implemented by developing countries facing severe balance of payments problems may, unintentionally, discriminate against foreign-based financial institutions.

The link between trade in banking and financial services and the developing country debt situation warrants specific mention. In recent times, the Government of Brazil expelled Mellon Bank of the United States because it had reportedly refused to endorse the roll-over of some US$150 million in short-term debt owed to it by Brazil. The Government of the Philippines was later reported to be considering similar action against another US bank with three branches in the Philippines. There is a widespread developing country view that foreign banks' policies and practices contributed to the debt problem and that, in spite of this, foreign banks are not now bearing an adequate share of the cost of resolving this problem. This will affect developing country attitudes towards foreign banks and make trade in services negotiations in banking more difficult than they otherwise would have been. On the other hand, foreign banks have to be part of the solution and most developing countries realise this. In addition to resumed bank lending, foreign banks have a role to play in strengthening domestic financial systems.

Many of the measures introduced by developing countries in the name of monetary policy will reflect entirely legitimate concerns -- concerns which, in a different context, are manifested by growing attention in developed countries to the challenge which financial deregulation can pose for monetary targeting, exchange rate management and the balanced transfer of human and physical resources into the financial services sector. At the same time, some measures will not reflect legitimate concerns. Moreover, many restrictive measures, whatever their underlying motivation, will run the risk of reducing the efficiency of domestic banking and financial services while creating trade distortions through discriminatory application.

Where LDC financial market deregulation (as distinct from liberalisation in removing discriminatory treatment of foreign banks) affects cross-border capital movements, provision will be needed for possible disruptive effects on the domestic economy. A safeguard provision is included in the OECD Code of Liberalisation of Capital Movements (Article 7) when justified by a Member's economic and financial situation and when invoked in a non-discriminatory way.

iii) Economic development

Banking and financial services are seen by most developing countries as part of their infrastructure and therefore warranting control for political reasons. Justification for such control may also be seen to stem from the tendency in developing countries for banks, whatever their status, to show a greater interest in the modern and urban sector than in the rural sector and small business. This is reflected by the continued existence of unofficial financial markets charging exorbitant rates to the traditional sector. The achievement of developmental goals through banking and financial services is likely to be approached in markedly different ways among LDCs, however, as witnessed by the contrasting experience of India and the Republic of Korea.

-- In India, since 1955 when the Imperial Bank of India was nationalised, banking has been used as an instrument of social change. Extensive nationalisation of domestic banking has enabled the Government to issue policy directives to stimulate the provision of finance to the small-scale sector and rural areas. State-owned banks have to lend, at less than market rates of interest, 40 per cent of their total advances to agriculture and small-scale enterprises assigned priority by the Government. While nationalising commercial banking, foreign banks were left untouched. They were permitted to continue their activities as before but their future expansion of activities was halted. In the process, foreign banks have been exempted from the obligations placed on Indian banks in regard to various lending and branch expansion requirements. Accordingly, in authorising new branch offices of foreign banks consideration is given to the specialised services which they can render, particularly in international loans, syndications and investment. Indian policy thus seeks to foster a complementary, if highly prescribed, role for foreign banks.

-- In contrast, in the Republic of Korea, as noted earlier, foreign banks are required to abide by regulations formerly applicable only to domestic banks, including a requirement that 25 per cent of foreign banks' loans must be made to small or medium-sized companies. In the absence of full national treatment this can create difficulties for foreign banks. Korean banks can foreclose

47

on mortgages taken as collateral when lending to small companies. Foreign banks can take mortgages as collateral but are not permitted to foreclose on them.

iv) Infant industry protection

Many of the policy measures already referred to will also have been prompted by concerns to shield the domestic banking industry from the full force of foreign competition. Indeed, such concerns will in many cases have played a greater role than those related to prudential control or monetary policy. Since the end of the Second World War, developing country banking policy has been directed chiefly to nurturing and promoting national financial institutions. Support for the domestic industry has thus gathered momentum in the course of decolonisation and as a corollary to the internationalisation of banking.

Given the long-lasting nature of many of the policy instruments employed, the relative sophistication of some developing country banking systems, and the multiple purpose of government controls, the measures adopted will often correspond only very approximately to "infant industry" protection. In some of the more advanced developing countries, the domestic currency market has been recognised as a lucrative business to be restricted, on a continuing basis, to domestic interests. Many developing countries will nevertheless be influenced by infant industry type considerations and may be motivated by the potential comparative advantage which they perceive in their indigenous banking industry. This may reflect the essentially labour-intensive nature of the distribution side of banking and financial services (requiring close personal contacts and detailed knowledge of local markets) but also the scope for economies of scale as information technology spreads to the production side of LDC banking (the creation of financial services).

Developing countries will also be influenced by the advantages which foreign-based multinational banks are seen to enjoy. These advantages, it may be felt, could enable foreign banks, if unchecked, to dominate the domestic industry and, through it, important aspects of economic policy. In addition to the operating flexibility referred to earlier, multinational banks' competitive edge will derive from their access to highly trained personnel, their superior information base, their ability to absorb new technology and their scope to cross-subsidise local financial services through their foreign parents. The result, it is suggested, is a higher level of profitability for foreign-based than for domestic banks.

Many developing countries have been characterised as having banking policies which reflect infant industry considerations (particular attention having been directed to Brazil, India, Kenya, Malaysia, Mexico, Nigeria, Republic of Korea, Thailand and Venezuela).

-- In Brazil, protection against foreign banks has been in operation since 1964 and is fully consistent with that country's policy of industrial development. There, as in India, foreign banks' activities are closely restricted except where specific interests are served. Discriminatory tax regimes may also apply -- as in India where foreign banks are taxed at 75.25 per cent as opposed to a 60 per cent tax for Indian banks. In Malaysia, a foreign firm wishing to borrow more than M$500 000 must give at least half its business to indigenous banks. There may also be limitations on access to deposits -- as in Venezuela where foreign banks cannot accept Government demand deposits or savings deposits of residents.

Apart from the potential costs to efficiency, two important areas of uncertainty are associated with infant industry type considerations. The first relates to levels of profitability. In the eleven LDCs for which country studies were conducted there was a tendency for foreign banks to be more profitable than local banks. But this was not universally so; it did not apply in Brazil, Ivory Coast and Singapore, nor in the Republic of Korea for the period 1970 to 1980. In short, firm conclusions cannot be drawn about the likelihood of multinational bank expansion on the basis of profitability. Secondly, and more fundamentally, it might be suggested that a complementarity exists between domestic and foreign banks and that the competitive threat of foreign banks is therefore exaggerated. As noted earlier, the extent of foreign banks' involvement in LDC retail banking does appear to have been relatively modest. This in turn, however, raises an important question: Is this apparent separation of functions a reflection of banks having taken their preferred areas of specialisation (with foreign banks content to concentrate on what they do best) or is the limited role of foreign banks in retail business simply the result of extensive governmental restrictions in that sector? If it is accepted that discriminatory policies are, at least in part, a contributory factor then important implications will follow for the process of trade expansion.

2. Insurance

a. Introduction

Consideration of developing country concerns in the area of insurance reveals a number of shared characteristics with the banking and financial services sector: a high degree of dependence in many LDCs on insurance services provided by foreign-based or controlled insurers, in turn reflecting underlying economic constraints; the need to clearly distinguish the process of liberalisation from the preservation of regulations needed for fiduciary control and consumer protection; and the potentially important linkage between the insurance industry and macroeconomic management.

Characteristics also emerge, however, which are peculiar to the insurance sector and which may raise particularly sensitive issues, notably: the influence of social and cultural factors in many developing country regions on attitudes towards insurance services; and the possible scope to achieve a better balance within many LDCs between the forms of trade embodied, respectively, in insurance and reinsurance.

Scope for efficiency gains through a process of trade expansion is apparent. But these gains will need to be seen in the context of legitimate developing country concerns to nurture a viable domestic capacity in the insurance sector.

b. Sector Profile

The definition and scope of insurance activities used here will be relatively broad. To the basic function of providing policy-holders with financial protection against specific risk over a specified period will thus be added various related services such as risk analysis, loss prevention advice and savings and investment programmes. Trade in insurance is taken to include both international sales by non-established insurers and establishment business. The latter is frequently favoured by insurers, in improving their competitive position. Establishment, particularly through subsidiaries, may also be favoured by some host governments, in facilitating supervision of insurance activities and in fostering the indigenisation of local industries.

The nature of insurance activity in developing countries reveals a number of important characteristics.

i)   The share of life insurance in total insurance business of developing countries is, overall, significantly smaller than the corresponding share of business in other countries (although this does not apply, in particular, in India, the Republic of Korea, Taiwan and Zimbabwe). The lesser role played by life insurance in many developing countries reflects, in part, the relatively low disposable incomes in these countries, the low investment returns on life funds and the application of social security provisions in some countries. It also reflects, in widely differing developing country regions, deep-seated cultural and religious influences. Many millions of Moslems still regard insurance as contrary to the tenets of their faith; many ethnic groups within Asia regard buying life policies as unlucky; and in many African countries the role of life insurance is marginalised by customs of succession and family solidarity and by religious beliefs (64).

ii) Over the past three decades, nationals of developing countries have acquired control and management of domestic insurance companies and created national companies. In some cases this has prompted withdrawal of foreign-based insurers. In the 30 years to 1981 British insurers withdrew operations from 18 African and 10 Asian countries (65). More commonly, however, developing country indigenisation has led multinational insurers to adapt the nature of their operations. Most significantly, this has contributed to the increased importance of subsidiaries relative to branches in the overseas activities of multinational insurance companies. The share

50

of branches in the overseas business of French insurance companies fell from 52 to 28 per cent between 1972 and 1984 (66). The extent of indigenisation has not, however, been uniform as between developing country regions. In Arab countries, while the role of foreign companies in insurance has been reduced in the last two decades, the proportion of foreign to total companies operating in the Arab region as a whole is still far higher (66 per cent) than in other developing country regions (Latin America, 27 per cent; Africa, 31 per cent; Asia, 44 per cent). In Saudi Arabia only foreign insurers operate because of Islamic objections to local incorporation of insurance enterprises. The impact of indigenisation can also be seen in specific sectors. For example, while developing countries in the past tended to insure their exports and imports with insurance institutions located in developed countries, most have now begun to conduct insurance of their imports within their own countries.

iii) Insurers in most developing countries have a high dependence on international reinsurance services. This is, in part, the corollary of moves to national control of insurance and reduced reliance on foreign-based insurers. In developing country markets served exclusively by domestic insurers, a large volume of outward reinsurance is observed. This is particularly marked in the case of Morocco where only locally owned or government companies operate. In contrast, in Singapore where both foreign and domestic insurers operate, the low level of retention of primary insurance business by the domestic insurance companies is largely compensated for by the extensive retention levels of foreign insurers (67). Dependence on reinsurance is, in large measure, a reflection of the small size and undercapitalisation of many LDC firms together with the unbalanced portfolio of risk faced by many developing countries. Insurance demand in developing countries is frequently concentrated on low-expense coverage (such as motor vehicle insurance), high-risk coverage (such as aircraft insurance), and large-risk coverage. A recent survey of 64 developing countries revealed 43 as having a reinsurance ratio (one minus the ratio of net premium to gross premium) greater than 30 per cent (68). Increasing resort to reinsurance by developing countries has been a major factor in the proliferation of this business in recent years. Some 75 per cent of the 376 professional reinsurance companies operating in the world have existed for under 25 years (69).

In insurance underwriting, the identification of risks and the assessment of their value often calls for considerable technical expertise. Engineers, lawyers, physicians and other technicians must classify risks, which must then be analysed by actuaries for the statistical properties of losses and claims. Developing country indigenisation notwithstanding, the providers of this and other insurance services are, predominantly, companies based in developed countries. Some expansion of LDC-based enterprises has occurred, however, through the establishment of subsidiaries in major insurance markets and the formation of regional bodies, such as the Arab Reinsurance and Insurance Group.

It is within the developed countries that the bulk of insurance business is produced. In 1985, developing countries accounted for 5.1 per cent of world premiums (4.5 per cent in respect of life insurance and 5.6 per cent for general or non-life insurance) (70). Nevertheless, the percentage of world premium produced by developing countries is estimated to have doubled since 1950. Particularly rapid growth was experienced in 1985 in Brazil, the Republic of Korea, Chile, Venezuela, Taiwan, Colombia and Guatemala. (The countries of Africa all witnessed either very low or negative growth). In the past six years, the Republic of Korea's world ranking in insurance business has increased from 23rd to 11th.

The important linkages between the insurance industry and economic activity involve a two-way process, reflecting the dependence of the insurance sector on underlying economic conditions but also the contribution which the insurance industry, in turn, can make towards economic growth and development.

As already observed, factors such as low disposable income in developing countries have an important bearing on the volume of insurance business. The UNCTAD has noted that efforts to increase premium incomes and to provide the basis for more solid risk-bearing capacity in developing countries have often been thwarted by the constraints of balance of payments and external debt problems which have depressed insurance demand (71). The impressive growth of the Korean insurance industry -- in line with the pace of economic growth -- can be seen as the obverse of the constraints facing many LDCs. In fact, the growth of insurance business in Korea has been seen more as a reflection of the rapid growth in demand for financial savings since 1980 than for insurance as such (72).

At the international level, the demand for insurance is seen to be highly income elastic and responsive to fluctuations of the economic cycle. Real premium income declined markedly during the global recession of 1974-1975 and again from the late 1970s to the mid 1980s (witnessing a strong recovery in 1985, with real growth of some 12 per cent). The crucial role of interest rate fluctuation, and associated movement in insurance premiums, in insurance cycles may have implications for the scope for regulatory controls to smooth swings in the cycle. It has been observed that rising interest rates have led to declining profitability as insurance companies aggressively cut premiums as an offset to expected gains in investment income (73).

An approximate measure of the extent of insurance within a country can be obtained from the ratio of premiums to gross domestic product. For the 64 developing countries referred to earlier, this figure was 1.6 per cent in 1983-1984, compared with an average value of 4.5 per cent for the US, Canada and Western Europe. Two qualifications are called for, however. First, there are wide disparities among LDCs [ranging (on a basis of GNP) from 0.72 per cent for Pakistan to 6.92 per cent for the Republic of Korea]. Second, the economic significance of insurance for developing countries is not susceptible to a single quantitative measure.

The importance of insurance to the trade and development process was acknowledged at the 1st session of UNCTAD in 1964 when it was formally noted that "a sound national insurance and reinsurance market is an essential characteristic of economic growth" (74). While insurance can be a final product (when, for example, providing family income in the case of disablement) it plays perhaps its major economic role as an intermediate service -- facilitating the flow of goods and services; promoting and channelling savings; and encouraging new technologies.

It has been suggested that the benefits of insurance are of even more critical importance to developing countries than to developed countries given that LDCs face relatively greater risks together with serious constraints on the development process through lack of investible capital and savings (75). Specific aspects of insurance may also be of particular importance to developing countries. For example, maritime fraud, which is spreading, is considered to affect particularly the interests of developing countries and their insurers.

Particular mention should be made of catastrophe insurance, of potentially major importance to developing countries. This is reflected in two recent illustrations:

-- The Mexico earthquake of September 1985 (estimated to have cost up to US$ 3000 million) has prompted many LDCs to consider the economic determinants for an optimum domestic insurance and reinsurance policy;

-- In the course of the Gulf War, a number of Arab countries (Saudi Arabia, Kuwait, Bahrain, Qatar, UAE and Oman) agreed on a compensation scheme to replace any oil shipped from their ports and lost as a result of military action.

c. Developing Country Concerns

Before looking at the nature of developing country concerns in the area of insurance, it may be useful to recall briefly the trade-related measures which those concerns prompt. They are likely to range over the following:

-- Limitations on placing insurance abroad.

-- State monopoly of all insurance.

-- Prohibition on establishment by foreign insurers of new subsidiaries and/or branches.

-- Requirement for entry through joint venture with local majority.

-- Limits on foreign equity.

-- Restrictions on field of activity.

-- Requirements to place government business with local insurers.

-- Proportion of transport or cargo insurance to be placed with local insurers.

-- Proportion of insurance to be ceded to national reinsurance company.

-- Restrictions on remittances by ceding insurers or reinsurers.

-- Discriminatory taxation.

-- Discriminatory capital requirements.

-- Restrictions on profit remittances.

The most common measures appear to be those relating to cross-border trade and establishment, and those applied to the two areas of insurance which are essentially international -- reinsurance and international transport or cargo insurance. It is possible, however, that lack of transparency leads to an understatement of measures in some areas (such as discriminatory capital and deposit requirements).

Four areas of developing country concern will be considered, corresponding broadly to those identified in respect of banking and financial services. The concerns -- consumer protection, balance of payments constraints, economic development and infant industry support -- are listed with a progressively increasing developing country focus although none of the concerns is unique to LDCs. Underlying each of the concerns, particularly that related to infant industry considerations, is likely to be a sense of dependency on insurance services provided by foreign-based or controlled insurers. Thus while dependency is not discussed as a separate issue it will be seen to be an important and recurring underlying motivation for developing country policies in the field of insurance.

i) Consumer protection

The need to protect consumers -- who, with imperfect knowledge, may have difficulty in assessing insurance services -- is widely recognised as providing a case for fiduciary regulation aimed at ensuring solvency, reliability, prudence and legal accountability.

One of the most difficult issues arising with respect to fiduciary regulation concerns the question of discriminatory application as between foreign-based and local insurers. While comprehensive data are lacking, it is widely suggested that a number of countries (developed and developing) impose differential capital requirements, particularly in the form of higher initial deposits for foreign-based insurers. Furthermore, in cases where deposit requirements appear to be equivalent, account generally is not taken of the reserves which foreign parent companies generally maintain in their country of origin.

The principal argument advanced in support of differential treatment is that insurance businesses which have the greater part of their assets in a foreign country cannot be subject to the same degree of control as those predominantly based in the host country. The response to this argument is closely linked to the question of the degree of "foreigness" of the insurers concerned. There appears to be no clear case for any differentiation in measures concerning, respectively, domestic companies and foreign subsidiaries. Once locally established as a subsidiary an insurance company has the same obligations and is subject to the same safeguards as a domestic company. The case of foreign branches is likely to be somewhat less clear as supervisory authorities will generally have less certain control. Nevertheless, it has been suggested that the experience of countries in which domestic operations and foreign branch operations are regulated similarly indicates that the additional risk to policy-holders of dealing with foreign companies is negligible (76).

The preceding discussion of fiduciary regulation relates essentially to direct insurance. It is important to note, however, that while the direct sector is subject to widespread regulation aimed at ensuring solvency and stability, the same degree of fiduciary regulation is not present in the reinsurance sector. This has occurred despite, or perhaps because of, the rapid growth in recent years of reinsurance coverage by foreign reinsurers. It has been observed by the UNCTAD secretariat that the proliferation of reinsurers in recent times has brought with it many serious problems and that the insurance markets in developing countries have become particularly vulnerable to upheavals involving the financial stability of international reinsurers. This has prompted the UNCTAD secretariat to suggest certain measures to ensure that ceded reinsurance is offered only by credible and solvent reinsurers. In discussion of insurance issues within OECD it has been stressed that reinsurance security and credibility depend not so much on improved control but on improved information which the ceding company should seek and the reinsurer should readily provide.

ii) Balance of payments constraints

A specific and readily identifiable balance of payments effect of trade in insurance services arises from the insurance of transportation risks when insurance is bought in the exporting market. This practice is believed to result in substantial foreign exchange expenditure for many developing countries and has prompted the widespread adoption of measures to stimulate the placement of international transport or cargo insurance with domestic insurers.

More broadly, however, balance of payments considerations are likely to be invoked in support of the promotion of LDC domestic insurance capacity across the whole range of the sector. It has thus been suggested by the UNCTAD that:

"The decision to produce internal insurance as opposed to importing external insurance or reinsurance should be viewed against the background of the critical shortage of foreign exchange that currently afflicts most developing countries and the relative scarcity of production factors. One dollar spent in imported insurance is one dollar less for the import of other goods and services whose domestic production cost might be higher than that of insurance" (77).

The case for promoting domestic insurance capacity on balance of payments grounds is, however, complicated by, in particular, three factors:

-- The outflow resulting from the investment abroad of premiums or reserve funds may over time be more than offset by an inflow against claims. Deficiencies in comparable statistics seriously hinder any assessment of the net balance of payments effect, particularly for developing countries.

-- The promotion of domestic insurance capacity involves a cost in terms of the use of domestic factors of production. Such costs -- which are likely to be higher in a complex area such as aviation insurance than in, say, life or fire insurance -- would need to be set against any savings of foreign exchange resulting from import replacement. The balance of payments argument cannot be invoked in support of reduced imports of insurance without consideration of alternative forms of import saving and the relative costs of domestic production in each of the activities considered.

-- As noted earlier, reduced reliance on foreign-based insurers is likely to lead to increased dependence on international reinsurance services. In this case, any gains through reduced foreign exchange outlays on direct insurance are likely to be significantly reduced.

Given the lack of reliable data on comparable reinsurance it is not possible to assess, comprehensively, the net effect of reinsurance transactions on the balance of payments of developing countries. While it appears to be agreed that a period of relatively low reinsurance premiums and liberal conditions has given way to a hardening of terms for reinsurance buyers, this will impact unevenly on different developing countries. International reinsurance transactions can result in net currency flows in either direction. If the total premiums ceded to the reinsurers exceed the commissions and losses to be paid and the reinsurance deposits to be constituted then a balance will be due to the reinsurers. The experience of developing countries reveals considerable diversity (78).

-- In India, for whom reinsurance is of particular importance, the import and export of reinsurance over the period 1976-1982 yielded a deficit in five years out of seven but a small net surplus over the period as a whole. In a number of developing countries major catastrophes have induced very large net inflows in particular years (Managua, US$ 1 000 million in 1972; Guatemala, US$ 750 million in 1976; and the Republic of Korea, US$ 46 million in 1980).

-- For the Arab countries, the import and export of reinsurance yielded a net outflow in all the years 1971-1980, producing a net balance of payments deficit of US$ 68 million for the period as whole (representing 12 per cent of the total written premiums of the market). Similarly, for the ASEAN countries, reinsurance has produced a significant net outward flow.

The perceived balance of payments costs of reinsurance have prompted a range of measures in many developing countries to encourage increased retention in the domestic market. Some countries resort to discriminatory taxation to discourage reinsurance abroad and place restrictions on the remittance of funds between the ceding company and the reinsurer. In Israel, for example, a tax of 15 per cent is applied on all reinsurance premiums transferred abroad. Other countries have pursued a policy of enforced mergers of domestic insurance companies with the aim of increasing the average size of insurance concerns. The most common degree of control over outward reinsurance is the requirement that local insurers should cede a stipulated portion of each risk to a domestic central reinsurance company. Each of these approaches will have implications for the efficiency of domestic insurance operations and the possible gains from trade expansion.

iii) Economic development

Of the economic linkages spreading out from insurance two are of particular importance for developing countries: capital mobilisation and support for specific sectors of activity.

Capital mobilisation: The time lag between the collection of premiums and the settlement of claims permits the investment of insurance funds by the industry. In general or non-life insurance, funds tend to be in the range of 120 to 140 per cent of annual premiums. In life insurance, amounts so mobilised are relatively more important as an implicit savings component is included in premiums. Insurers thus become a potentially important financial agent in many countries and a key investment mechanism, particularly in property and development projects.

To help foster the insurance industry's capital mobilisation role, a number of developing countries have taken steps to develop the life insurance sector of the industry (notwithstanding the inherent constraints facing life insurance in many LDCs). Bangladesh, Argentina and Thailand have each recently introduced new categories of life insurance. In the 1960s, in order to help finance its ambitious economic growth plans, the government of the Republic of Korea introduced various measures to encourage the savings function of life insurance companies.

More generally, concerns to foster capital mobilisation have led to calls for funds and technical reserves of insurance companies to be invested in the country where the premium arises (79). While, in practice, the resulting constraints imposed on insurers may not be particularly onerous they can nevertheless be a source of inefficiency. The underlying rationale for such constraints stems from a perception in developing countries that foreign-based insurers tend to invest their funds in the country of their head office or other high-yielding capital markets. While it has been suggested that such an investment practice is neither rational (given capital scarcity and the scope for high-yielding investment in developing countries) nor in fact reflected in the respective investment portfolios of domestic and foreign-based insurers (80), the presence of foreign insurers is felt by many LDCs to bring an inherently unpredictable and unstable environment for the supply of investment funds.

In any further consideration of this question an important distinction might be drawn between the requirement, consistent with prudent insurance practice, that a reasonable proportion of premiums historically required to cover claims be kept in the country where the risks are covered and any additional requirement for the retention of profits.

Sectoral support: The need to better integrate insurance transactions in the development process has been widely recognised, including at a Third World Insurance Congress held in Casablanca, Morocco, in 1984. Attention has been directed to insurance schemes of social and economic importance, such as agricultural and crop insurance, transportation insurance, catastrophe insurance and export credit insurance. Particular focus has been put on the agricultural sector given the scope for insurance to help facilitate new farming techniques, crop diversification and rural credit.

From a developing country perspective, agricultural insurance is frequently seen as supporting the contention that domestic insurance can take better care of domestic needs. It is thus claimed that the neglect of potential domestic demand for agricultural insurance in developing countries is attributable to the foreign traditions and patterns that insurance industries in these countries have inherited. Deficiencies in agricultural insurance have been identified, in particular, in Africa and in many Arab countries for whom the rural sector is of considerable importance (81).

In response to this situation, new or extended agricultural insurance programmes have been introduced recently in several developing countries (Bangladesh, Brazil, China, Colombia, Guyana, Paraguay and Zambia), many of them with direct public support.

-- Brazil's national crop insurance programme has survived with the aid of large government subsidies. In 1980, the subsidy from the central bank represented 58 per cent of the programme's total revenue.

Indeed, deficiencies in agricultural insurance in developing countries may be not so much the result of neglect of LDC interests by insurers based in industrialised countries but rather a reflection of the need for extensive governmental support in this field of insurance. The experience of both developed and developing countries thus suggests that there are some categories of business which private companies (whether foreign-based or domestic) may be unable or unwilling to transact. With few exceptions, farmers have been unwilling to pay the full cost of all-risk crop insurance. Studies in respect of Mexico indicate that crop insurance for maize and beans would require a subsidy of two-thirds or more of the total cost to be attractive to farmers. Nevertheless, while many agricultural insurance schemes have the character of public risk policies (thus going beyond the immediate field of trade) experience in some countries (notably in the Sao Paulo and Minas Gerais states of Brazil) has identified particular schemes that could act as a bridgehead for the future transfer of responsibility for crop insurance from the government to private insurers (82).

Government involvement, of a different nature, may also be a feature of the interaction between insurance services and manufacturing activity. It is understood that in <u>the Republic of Korea</u> the government has imposed various restrictions on companies' asset management, in order to channel their funds to finance designated strategic industrial sectors.

iv) Infant industry support

Many, if not all, of the measures that have been referred to so far have been invoked in order to foster the fledgling domestic insurance industries of developing countries. A study of services trade by authorities in <u>India</u> identifies the desire to protect local companies against foreign competition as the foremost reason for barriers against foreign entry in insurance business (83). Many LDCs have considered that insurance institutions locally incorporated are an essential element of their economic independence and hence worthy of special encouragement. Infant industry-type support is designed to develop potential comparative advantage through a "learning-by-doing" process and to obviate the clear weaknesses of developing country insurance institutions and a perceived LDC vulnerability in this sector.

<u>Developing country disabilities</u>: Developing country weaknesses in insurance are partly a reflection of specific disabilities of domestic insurance companies. More fundamentally, however, they reflect underlying economic constraints. The nature of weakness in the insurance sector in developing countries thus precludes ready generalisation -- it will depend on the degree and nature of linkage between the local insurance industry and foreign insurers and, most importantly, on the economic circumstances of the country in question.

Part IB of this document identifies four particular areas of LDC weakness -- corresponding closely to those elements on which comparative advantage in insurance is believed to depend. Moreover, in the years ahead the global nature of insurance is likely to reflect the far-reaching technical changes taking place in the industry -- changes that will provide a further challenge to developing countries in this sector. The insurance industry (with masses of data, complex calculations and standardised documentation) lends itself readily to computerisation. The internationalisation of insurance is thus likely to grow with the adoption of information-based technologies. Information technology is enabling risk to become a tradable commodity, as witnessed by the recent joint venture between SWIFT and I.P. Sharp in which the SWIFT network will provide global risk monitoring and management services.

<u>Developing country vulnerability</u>: The weaknesses facing developing countries in the insurance sector are widely perceived as bringing with them significant vulnerability. One immediate consequence, already noted, is the heavy dependence on reinsurance. Beyond this, a number of specific forms of vulnerability are commonly referred to.

-- Developing countries are, arguably, inherently more vulnerable to risk than developed countries, whether through natural circumstances, as development pushes into hitherto sparsely inhabited areas, or through the scale of industrial projects relative to GNP. It has also been said that developed countries have sometimes been more successful in transferring technology to LDCs than they have been in providing the means of coping with the risks associated with this technology (84).

-- Dependency on insurance from overseas or from foreign-based companies may, in extreme circumstances, bring with it a risk that insurance cover will be denied. In the event of war or major civil upheaval involving developing countries, the insurance and reinsurance markets of developed countries may consider it prudent to withdraw cover of, for example, marine and aviation risk (85). It is indeed sometimes argued that security considerations warrant the development of a domestic insurance capacity regardless of considerations of potential comparative advantage.

Policy response: In pursuing infant industry-type policies developing countries will hope that by encouraging domestic producers they will become as efficient as foreign insurers more quickly than would otherwise be the case. But in rationalising such policies, efficiency arguments are frequently accompanied by appeals to equity (86).

-- The ASEAN Insurance Commissioners have agreed that "foreign companies should not compete for the conventional types of business and should allow domestic insurers a more equitable share of the market".

-- A meeting to discuss Latin American interests in insurance (Federacion Interamericana de Empresas de Seguros, La Paz, 1984) concluded that: "If big markets step into small markets, the latter will perish".

The desire to achieve some degree of self-sufficiency in insurance has thus been a pervasive feature of developing country policy -- underpinning the promotion of domestic insurance in the post-independence period and, more recently, providing a focus for the Republic of Korea's initial resistance to United States' requests for access to the insurance market. It is perhaps significant, however, that in ultimately granting access to the domestic insurance market Korean authorities acknowledged the efficiency gains this might bring. It is also reported that in respect of business emanating from TNCs strict policies that such business be transacted in the country where the risk is situated have recently been relaxed in a number of LDCs. Such policy shifts may, in part, reflect an acknowledgement that infant industry-type policies cannot be pursued without a cost.

3. Tourism and Travel

a. Introduction

A discussion of developing country interests in tourism and travel reveals a number of inherent contradictions in this area.

-- A field of activity which (in IMF terms) yields a surplus for developing countries, overall, and a deficit for developed countries, and where many LDCs have important natural advantages, it is nevertheless a field in which the industrialised countries play the major role.

-- Many of the policy measures which impinge on the tourism industry are often motivated by underlying concerns quite dissociated from it, while some measures of explicit support for the local tourism industry can be counterproductive, acting as a form of export limitation.

-- The wide-ranging nature which itself contributes to the economic importance of tourism and travel may require that the exact scope and delineation of the sector be agreed upon in the course of Uruguay Round negotiations.

b. Sector Profile

Tourism is the business of servicing travellers, both international and domestic. It is composed of a coalition of diverse industries often producing only part of their output for final, tourism, demand. Activities range over transport, accommodation, food preparation, travel agency and tour facilities, with linkages spreading directly into areas such as construction, data processing and insurance, and beyond these into most fields of economic activity. The linkage to international transport is particularly strong, with important implications for developing country dependence. (Travel and airline activity will be considered here, however, only insofar as they relate directly to tourism). As noted earlier, trade in tourism will be regarded as encompassing both the purchases by individual tourists and the activities of tourism enterprises.

Many developing countries, often faced with poor commodity prices and diminished export prospects, have directed increasing attention to tourism as a source of foreign exchange. In 1985, some 15 developing countries had travel income in excess of US$ 500 million. At the extreme, for nine small island developing countries gross receipts from tourism exceed the combined total of visible exports (87).

As noted earlier, while a number of developing countries are major participants in international tourism, it is the industrialised countries that account for the bulk of tourist "arrivals" and international receipts and that provide the base for most international tourism enterprises. In the international hotel industry some 72 multinational corporations based in developed countries play a major role, with US hotels earning foreign receipts of some US$ 2.3 billion in 1981.

The larger the absolute size of the hotel sector in any particular country, the lower the foreign participation rate in the provision of accommodation is likely to be. Small tourism sectors in developing countries are more likely therefore to be dependent on foreign-associated hotel companies. Unlike the situation in manufacturing, foreign direct investment is not the main method of multinational involvement in hotel companies -- management contracts and franchise agreements assuming greater importance (88).

Service activities, generally, are often regarded as being relatively less affected by cycles of economic activity than merchandise trade. This may also hold true for tourism and travel. Nevertheless, international tourism has shown significant responsiveness to developments in the world economy. After 25 years of steady growth, the aftermath of the first oil shock brought a marked drop in international tourist receipts in 1974. Following a subsequent period of rapid growth, tourist activity again slowed markedly in the early 1980s (89). At the same time, tourism has shown a marked sensitivity to differing geographic growth patterns. Reflecting, in part, the growing importance of business travellers gravitating towards countries with high economic growth, tourist "arrivals" in Asia grew by 17 per cent from 1960 to 1985, compared with 3.6 per cent in North America and 6.1 per cent in Europe. In addition, tourist flows are highly sensitive to exchange rate fluctuations and to developments in the areas of security and public health.

The diverse linkages spreading out from tourism are of dual significance. Firstly, they are important for the tourism sector itself; the ability to construct a comprehensive package of related services being a key to establishing a competitive position. This is clearly reflected in the activities of the international tourism enterprises. At the same time, the inability to provide an effective package can inhibit tourism development in widely differing developing countries whether because of poor internal transport services (as in Indonesia), or because of lack of water and basic infrastructure (as in Kiribati) (90). Secondly, the linkages from tourism are a reflection of the sector's potential economic impact. While a measure of the net social gain from tourism is extremely difficult, as discussed earlier, some indication of the sector's impact can be derived from input-output statistics.

Tourism is sometimes expected to become a leading sector, generating rapid overall economic growth as a variant of the economic enclave. This objective is rarely likely to be attained, however, unless tourism is part of a complex of industries. The important spread effects of tourism emphasize the need for an integration of this sector with other aspects of economic development and for the avoidance of policies which serve, often incidentally, to discriminate against it. It seems, however, that, notwithstanding a tendency towards government involvement in LDC tourism activities, only a minority of countries have made a conscious effort to bring about greater integration of such activities with the rest of the economy.

c. Developing Country Concerns

The nature of developing country concerns will depend on the individual country's stage of development and its reliance on tourism earnings. Four broad categories of developing country concern will be distinguished: first, those relating essentially to underlying balance of payments constraints, often incidental to tourism and which developing countries may be able to address through unilateral action; second, concerns related to environmental and cultural interests which raise "public good" considerations; third, concerns related to the development of tourism (including infant industry-type considerations), where domestic action by LDCs may need to be accompanied by measures of international co-operation; and finally, concerns related to barriers erected by other countries against tourism trade, whether at the level of the enterprise or the individual traveller.

i) Balance of payments concerns

The first item listed under this heading relates to the outward movement of nationals (the "import" of tourism), the remainder concern the provision of services by tourism enterprises.

Residents' Overseas Travel: As noted above, while developing countries, overall, have a surplus on tourism trade (and developed countries a deficit), a significant number of LDCs have tourism deficits and are concerned by the size of their tourism debits.

In response to these debits a large number of developing, as well as developed, countries resort to various measures to discourage overseas travel by their residents. These may be likened to import quota-type measures (as with limits to the amount of foreign currency a resident may take abroad or items a returning resident may import free of duty); import duty-type measures (as with departure taxes); and import licence-type requirements (as with exit permits). The overall scale of these measures is widely acknowledged; more than 100 countries impose restrictions limiting the amount of currency their citizens may purchase for travel abroad (91). Among developing countries it is difficult, however, to discern any clear trend.

-- Nigeria and Cameroon have recently increased the currency allowance for residents travelling abroad and India has relaxed measures affecting residents' overseas travel. However, Brazil has introduced a 25 per cent tax on the cost of travel tickets purchased by residents travelling abroad, while Singapore authorities have expressed concern about steep increases in exit taxes in Indonesia and Thailand (92).

Income Remittances: Developing countries that are hosts to foreign-associated travel agents, tour operators, airlines or hotels will be concerned to maximise tourism revenues and minimise foreign currency outlays in respect of overseas earnings and management, franchise and licensing fees. As a reflection of this concern, restrictions may be placed on the employment of foreign personnel. In addition, a number of developing countries have been identified as having controls on access to foreign exchange needed to remit earnings or management fees in the hotel industry (in particular, Brazil, Chile, Dominican Republic, Egypt, Republic of Korea, Mexico, Peru and Taiwan). This concern is linked to dependency considerations which will be discussed later.

Import Leakage: A closely related concern is that arising from the relatively high import content of tourism services in many countries. While it may be observed that imports can be an important contributor to economic growth and that, imports notwithstanding, tourism provides net benefits to LDCs, the import component of tourism will nevertheless be seen as a drain on income. This is likely to apply particularly to smaller developing countries unable to produce a wide range of inputs. Some 51 per cent of tourist expenditure in the Seychelles is estimated to be on imported inputs (93). More economically diversified LDCs (and developed countries) also experience import leakage, if to a lesser extent.

-- The ratio of imports to total earnings from tourism for Singapore is estimated to be 31 per cent. Viewed more broadly, total import requirements to satisfy both tourism final demand as well as intermediate inputs is estimated at 3.1 per cent of Singapore's total imports of goods and services in 1979 (94).

Field studies by the United Nations Centre on Transnational Corporations suggest that some 10-20 per cent of current purchases and 20-60 per cent of capital goods are obtained through the central purchasing departments of multinational-associated hotels in developing countries.

In an attempt to reduce import leakage (and promote local manufacturing industry) some seven LDCs have been identified as having imposed restrictions on the import of hotel supplies (Argentina, Bangladesh, Barbados, Brazil, India, Mexico and Nigeria) (95). In India hotels are allowed to import provisions or machinery according to the foreign exchange they earn from their clients.

ii) "Public Goods" (Environmental and cultural integrity)

Government regulations to protect the environment and promote cultural integrity relate essentially to "public goods" or "externalities".

Environmental concerns can raise key questions for those numerous developing countries whose tourism is resource-based and where large numbers of foreign visitors can impose significant strains on natural physical endowments. As noted earlier, while the operating basis of multinational tourism enterprises may not always be compatible with the environmental interests of the host country, such enterprises have a strong long-term interest in recognising and avoiding any such incompatibility.

Cultural considerations are likely to be equally compelling (and, as with environmental concerns, for developed and developing countries alike). The careful balance required in enabling tourists to appreciate indigenous culture while at the same time preserving that culture's integrity is illustrated in the case of Indonesia. To protect Balinese religious, cultural and social life, Indonesian authorities have decided that tourism should be "contained" in one resort area with active Government involvement in land acquisition and the provision of utilities (96).

Environmental and cultural concerns will bear importantly on the question of possible "exceptions" to a liberalisation process.

iii) Tourism industry development

In addition to directly addressing the specific concerns listed, some of the measures described under points (i) and (ii) above may also be invoked by developing (and developed) countries on industry support grounds. (For example, discouraging nationals from travelling abroad may be presented as helping to support domestic tourism as well as saving foreign exchange). The concern to foster the domestic tourism industry (and, in particular, national enterprises) will in turn be called on in support of broad policy measures which are likely to affect access and establishment of foreign-associated tourism businesses. Measures to promote nationally controlled enterprises will be considered first before turning to more broad-based support for tourism generally, although the distinction between the two sets of measures may be difficult to draw in practice.

Infant industry-type concerns of developing countries are likely to reflect two closely related goals: to realise potential comparative advantage in tourism and to reduce a perceived dependency on foreign-associated enterprises.

Developing countries are likely to be particularly dependent on large tour operators dealing in mass tourism and whose operations may affect the net foreign exchange earnings of the host country. Pre-payment of charges, use of customer vouchers, and inter-company settlement of debts abroad rather than in the tourist receiving country may facilitate the evasion of foreign exchange controls and reduce the amount of foreign exchange accruing to the tourist receiving country. Such effects would be additional to those arising from "leakage" as discussed earlier.

The experience of Fiji suggests that the policies of the major air carriers can be a key determinant of the viability of the tourism industry, given the power to change the frequency and routing of scheduled flights (97) and the ability to restrict authorisation of non-scheduled flights. This example is illustrative of a constraint facing a large number of developing countries. The bilateral structure of the international airline industry may indeed have served to disadvantage the development of tourism in many developing countries -- particularly those relatively distant from major international travel paths.

"Self-reliance" in tourism is not, however, a meaningful goal for any country, developed or developing. There is thus no all-embracing policy approach for developing countries. The extent to which national tourism enterprises may be subject to specific support or protection will need to depend on the particular factor endowments of the developing country concerned, the alternative uses to which those endowments can be put and the cost of protection to the rest of the economy. Furthermore, the extent to which support is considered necessary is likely to depend also on the scope for mutually beneficial arrangements between host countries and foreign-associated enterprises concerning the transfer of skills and technology, the local sourcing of purchases and the indigenisation of employment.

Measures to help assist nationally controlled tourism enterprises include:

-- Requirements for minimum local equity participation in tourism ventures. This occurs, for example, in Maldives and Sri Lanka where foreign investment is more tightly restricted in small- than in large-scale projects and in Mexico where resort development companies are required to be 51 per cent locally owned. In India the maximum foreign equity permitted in hotel investment was raised recently from 40 to 51 per cent.

-- Restrictions on the ability of foreign-associated enterprises to solicit customers, advertise or sell directly to clients.

-- Direct support for local tourism enterprises. This may take the form of preferential treatment of national airlines in catering, fuelling, access to reservation systems, etc. (reported in Argentina, Brazil, Republic of Korea, Nigeria, Pakistan, Peru, Philippines, Taiwan, Thailand, and Venezuela); lack of equal access to local credit sources, particularly when scarce; and direct government incentives or subsidies.

The question of subsidies raises particularly difficult considerations. By helping to develop tourism-related facilities, subsidies can serve to promote trade by stimulating the flow of travellers. At the same time, if applied discriminately as between foreign and domestic enterprises, subsidies can distort trade at the tourism enterprise level. Tourism related support is likely, however, to extend into activities of particular sensitivity commonly regarded, in all countries, as legitimate areas of government support: basic infrastructure (covering possibly health and education, which can figure importantly in travellers' expenditure); environment protection; and cultural development. Further examination of this issue might draw on two elements: the need for an inventory of subsidies which do have distortive effects; and possible application of the national treatment principle which could, inter alia, require that projects eligible for subsidy be open to foreign contractors.

Further potential forms of assistance for the tourism industry (which would benefit both local and foreign enterprises) relate to:

-- Exchange rate policy. The establishment of a preferential exchange rate for visiting tourists (by enabling visitors to purchase tourism-related services more cheaply than can residents) could be regarded as the equivalent to "dumping". Practices will vary considerably, however, and the opposite situation may also apply. It is suggested that in Fiji and Jamaica foreign visitors subsidise the domestic population who are charged lower rates by hotels.

-- Taxation policy. In the Philippines hotels and tourist transport enterprises are granted a deduction from net taxable income equivalent to 50 per cent of total foreign exchange earned (98), while in Malaysia any hotel given a certificate of "pioneer status" is exempt from taxation for a period of 2 to 5 years (99).

iv) Tourism barriers

The final group of developing country concerns relates to barriers erected by other countries against trade in tourism, whether at the level of the individual traveller or of the tourism enterprise.

The important corollary of the earlier discussion of developing country restrictions on residents' overseas travel is that many developing countries are disadvantaged by measures that discourage outward movement of nationals from other countries (that is, by those countries' "import" restrictions). Many developing countries are likely to be particularly concerned at the implications for their tourism and other economic activities of restrictions imposed by other countries on the travel of their nationals because of public health or security considerations.

Developing countries, particularly those with the potential to set up tourism enterprises overseas, will also be disadvantaged by barriers erected in other countries against the establishment of tourist promotion offices and the activities of foreign-associated enterprises.

4. Maritime Transport

a. Introduction

In trying to identify the already diverse interests among different developing countries (whether reflecting shipowner, shipper or labour-sender interests), the maritime transport sector is found to be difficult to characterise in general terms:

-- It is an area of activity containing elements of both extensive regulation (as in liner conference trades) and relative freedom from government intervention (as in the bulk trades);

-- While sharing long established traditions and patterns of activity, shipping nevertheless is witnessing far-reaching technological and structural change as improved technologies become more widely diffused;

-- It is a sector that has experienced the parallel development both of areas of intense competition and of growing government intervention;

-- It has seen a major increase in the market share of developing countries, but an increase which is concentrated among a relatively small group of LDCs;

-- Finally, while international shipping is a sector where developing countries may derive some competitive strengths from the availability of low-cost labour, any assessment of the scale of this benefit is complicated by the high level of labour-migration in maritime transport and the employment of LDC seafarers by developed country flag operators.

As noted earlier, a significant feature of the maritime transport sector is the existence of an institutional arrangement (the United Nations Convention on a Code of Conduct for Liner Conferences) which specifically addresses developing country concerns.

b. Sector Profile

The varied nature of commodities transported by sea has led to the evolution of specialist ship types. General cargo is carried by liner services on board conventional cargo liners, cellular container vessels or roll-on roll-off vessels. Liner services are characterised by regularity of sailings and diversity of cargo. Bulk dry cargo, formerly handled by the general purpose tramp which plied for hire, is now carried almost exclusively by specialist bulk carriers.

The regular liner services have for some decades been "privately" regulated through liner conferences -- associations of carriers that have the purpose and/or effect of regulating rates, charges and conditions. Developing countries sought and finally obtained (by signature in 1974) a Convention on a Code of Conduct for Liner Conferences, which guarantees them a share of the liner conference trade. Bulk cargo shipping, which represents some 80 per cent of maritime transport, is relatively free of government restrictions. Shipping within national borders tends, under cabotage laws, to be restricted to domestic shipping companies.

The provision of maritime transport services has a strong and perhaps predominant "transborder" element -- as when a company sends its ships to load or deliver cargoes in foreign ports, without requiring establishment in each country. The question of establishment may nevertheless have particular importance in specific circumstances, where, for example:

-- Certain activities are reserved for the national flag but where, via establishment, foreigners have access to the operation of ships under that flag. (Access to cargoes, via access to flag). Nevertheless, in those markets which restrict access to cargo on the basis of flag, right of establishment may mean very little;

-- Foreign companies, particularly those engaged in multimodal transport, seek the right to invest in necessary port facilities and infrastructure. (Access to facilities).

In the context of the United Nations Convention on Liner Conferences, establishment may have particular significance for developing countries wishing to use, as their national line, the services of a foreign (usually developed country) line. To be eligible under the Convention, a national line must be established in the country in question.

The eventual definition agreed upon for "trade" in maritime services and, in particular, the treatment of inland transport movements associated with multimodal transport, will bear significantly on the extent to which establishment issues are an important focus of discussion.

From the perspective of developing countries, two characteristics of maritime transport might be seen as having particular significance.

i) Over the past two decades, major structural changes have taken place in shipping markets. In the bulk trades there has been a shift towards very large vessels, although the trend to giant oil tankers and "combination" (ore/oil) carriers appears to have been checked. In liner markets conventional tonnage has very extensively been replaced by container ships, significantly increasing productivity and enabling economies of scale in shipping general cargo to be obtained for the first time. A very large number of liner trades are now dominated by large fully-cellular ships. Shipping has become even more capital-intensive than before, significantly altering the balance of capital and labour inputs into shipping services (100). The growth of containerised vessels has, in turn, prompted four other important developments:

-- A reduction in the number of ports regularly served within individual receiving countries by overseas liner vessels, as shipowners seek to reap the economies of scale available from the capital-intensive terminals required to handle container vessels (101);

-- The introduction of round-the-world services, as operators seek economies of scale through the employment of container ships considerably larger than those used in end-to-end services;

-- The development of door-to-door (multimodal) transport, as technological and infrastructural adaptation to the container facilitates the movement of goods by more than one transport mode -- further blurring the distinction between ocean and land transport services;

-- The formation of consortia, as shipowners seek to share the high fixed costs associated with container services. Consortia may take a variety of forms and share no standard definition. Co-operation between members is usually centred on the physical operation of the fleet, while the individual component ships are still owned and crewed by the members individually. Members carry each other's containers on each other's ships under mutual slot charter arrangements. The degree of co-operation varies widely, from relatively loose arrangements to organisations so tight that they are in effect single units comparable with profit-making companies. In the process, the concept of "national line" has also become blurred.

ii) Despite pressures towards concentration in certain parts of the industry, a sustained role for innovative newcomers has been evident over the 1970s and 1980s. The power of liner conferences has thus been steadily eroded over this period. Whereas in the early seventies, conferences normally controlled in excess of 90 per cent of the liner cargo in particular trades, there are now very few cases where, on major routes, conferences control more than 80 per cent, and in a number of important trades the part transported by conferences is as low as 50 per cent or less. This is not to suggest, however, that unilateral rate-setting practices of conferences (where they have a strong market position) have ceased to be of concern.

The linkages between maritime transport and economic conditions involve a two-way process. The level and nature of activity in the shipping sector is critically dependent on broad trade and economic developments, while shipping itself is an important determinant of economic progress.

The declining importance over the last two decades of traditional general cargo ships and the rapid expansion in large oil tankers, dry bulk carriers and container ships is a direct reflection of the need to economise high labour and handling costs and of the importance of oil in the energy economy.

Since the early 1970s until recent times a number of factors contributed to excess capacity in most sectors of the shipping industry: a massive influx of tanker tonnage based on, in retrospect, unrealistic trade growth expectations; provision by governments in developed and some newly industrialising developing countries of financial incentives to shipbuilders; and lending by certain commercial banks against inflated hull values without adequate guaranteed employment. Largely as a consequence of the oversupply in tanker tonnage in the late seventies, an oversupply situation in dry bulk tonnage also developed as owners partly converted tanker orders to orders for bulk carriers and the large fleet of combination carriers was moved from oil to dry cargo. The oversupply situation also spread during the mid-eighties to container general cargo tonnage. The underlying reasons for these developments are, of course, not the same, but in general cargo too, the easy availability of credit facilities and insufficient equity were among the prime factors contributing to oversupply situations. More recently there has been a much more rigorous policy in extending credit to shipbuilders and the majority of banks have either withdrawn from this market or reduced their engagement to a minimum (102).

In response to the improved economic climate and the vigorous growth of world trade, seaborne movements increased by 6 per cent in 1988 as compared to a growth of 2 per cent in 1987 (103). This has led to a more balanced demand/supply equation although overcapacity persists in the liner trades and is sporadic in the bulk trades.

Shipping services contribute directly to the development process by fostering the expansion of trade. Technological change has played an important part in this process, in facilitating the shipment of particular products (such as liquefied natural gas). More generally, maritime transport can contribute to development by helping improve the foreign exchange situation and stimulating employment, while also fostering technology transfer and economic integration. Although hard to sustain, it has in fact been suggested, by the UNCTAD, that shipping is of relatively greater importance to developing than the developed countries, given limited scope for intra-regional land transport of trade among developing countries and a preponderance of raw materials and semi-finished products in LDC export composition. Without questioning the development role of shipping services, this proposition warrants qualification (arising, for example, from the intra-regional scope for land transport in Latin America and Africa, the growing importance of manufactures in developing country exports and the high dependence on shipping of many developed countries). The corollary of shipping's development role is that absence of adequate maritime transport can impose considerable costs. Tonga's fourth Five Year Plan (reflecting on operating problems of the Pacific Forum Line) noted that "the inadequacy and irregularity of shipping services, particularly in outer islands, results in large quantities of produce failing to reach internal and external markets" (104).

Two aspects of maritime transport's indirect contribution to economic development warrant specific mention: the links to other services and to shipbuilding. The overall efficiency of maritime transport depends importantly on interactions between a wide range of service activities, including banking, insurance, information, computer and communications services, brokerage, and handling and storage. Perhaps even more critical, however, is the linkage between shipping and shipbuilding. OECD shipbuilding capacity will have been reduced by some 51 per cent for the period 1975-1990 while capacity elsewhere will have increased by 42 per cent -- assistance to shipbuilding by OECD countries being designed not to maintain capacity but rather to foster restructuring by directing investment towards more profitable areas of shipbuilding activity.

The role of developing countries in maritime transport needs interpreting with some care. Overall, the developing market-economy countries achieved the target they set themselves at the end of the 1970s, of 20 per cent of world tonnage by the end of the decade, with three years to spare. This represents a very considerable increase over their global share of 8.5 per cent in 1975. LDC participation in the tanker, combination carrier and dry bulk sector has been particularly notable. Exceptionally rapid growth has been experienced by a number of Pacific Rim developing countries. The marked relative decline of world tonnage under OECD flags has been the result of both scrapping and flagging-out, although the traditional open registry countries have benefited less than a number of countries or dependent territories which have been providing facilities similar to those offered by the major open registry nations.

Within this broad assessment, however, a number of important qualifications are needed.

i)   First, the LDC share of world tonnage is concentrated among a relatively small number of countries. Apart from the open registry flags, very large fleets (over 4 million grt) are confined to nine developing countries (Brazil, China, Hong Kong, India, Iran, Republic of Korea, Philippines, Singapore and Taiwan). In Africa, only Egypt has a fleet over 1 million grt. Some 95 per cent of Africa's international trade is carried by sea, and 97.5 per cent of that maritime traffic is carried by foreign flag vessels. This experience is not, of course, confined to developing countries -- corresponding figures for Australia are some 99 and 96 per cent (105). The growing capital-intensity of shipping will nevertheless present a major challenge for most developing countries and only a very few LDCs are now in a position to acquire the necessary tonnage to be able to participate in an efficient manner in the liner conference's transport role. Notwithstanding the significant part played by a small number of developing countries in international shipping, most LDC vessels are old and outdated. The implications of capital-intensity for developing countries' role in maritime transport will be returned to later in this note.

ii) Second, over the most recent period, the Asian region continues to be the only substantial area of net growth for developing countries -- increased tonnage in 1987-88 in the Philippines (mainly as a result of a skilled use of the possibilities of bare-boat chartering) and, to a lesser extent, Republic of Korea offsetting tonnage reductions in Hong Kong. Several oil-producing states in the Gulf reduced their fleets as a result of reflagging, Iran being the only OPEC state to increase its fleet significantly.

iii)   Third, even where developing countries have increased their share of world tonnage, there are sub-sectors in which their participation remains limited, although opinions differ about the nature of participation. It is estimated by the United Nations Centre on Transnational Corporations (UNCTC) that 87 per cent of bauxite/alumina, 80 per cent of iron ore, and some two-thirds of phosphate and coal cargoes are accounted for by multinational enterprises (MNE) with vertically integrated operations (106). This assessment is not shared, however, by some maritime transport experts who question, in particular, the scale of the estimate for phosphate and the extent of MNE involvement (as distinct from developed country shipowner involvement) in coal shipment.

iv)   Finally, notwithstanding major gains in LDC tonnage shares, almost all developing countries continue to experience a large balance of payments deficit in shipping services. While the IMF "Shipment" item also includes air freight and the land component of some multimodal transport, it is made up predominantly of maritime freight and is therefore a reasonable proxy for the immediate balance of payments effect of maritime transport. Over the decade to 1985, only eight developing countries (for whom data are available) registered an improved balance in "shipment" (Argentina, Brazil, Chile, Equador, Israel, Republic of Korea, Philippines and Zambia). Moreover, the only two LDCs to show a significant surplus in "shipment" (Brazil and Korea) are among those developing countries that prefer to time-charter or lease vessels rather than to import shipping services. This practice has the effect of artificially reducing freight figures, because charter operations are recorded by the IMF under the "Other Transportation" item.

c. Aspects of Shipping Policy and the Regulatory Environment

Before examining the nature of developing country concerns, it may be useful to consider, briefly, the regulatory framework to which those concerns have contributed. Consideration will be given to the obstacles facing maritime transport before turning to the principles embodied in the UN Convention on a Code of Conduct for Liner Conferences (UN Liner Convention) and recent OECD instruments.

As pointed out in the annual report (1986) of the OECD Maritime Transport Committee (MTC), the problem of protectionism in international shipping is neither new nor confined to any one group of countries. Fleet development goals have prompted most if not all members of the international shipping community to engage in such practices. In particular, most nations possessing merchant fleets offer some kind of special financial assistance to their maritime industry to further their commercial and political interests. It seemes, however, that while OECD Member countries, for the most part, have

73

had limited freedom to introduce new direct measures developing countries have been less constrained (107). The past several decades have thus witnessed increased government involvement by LDCs (and state trading nations) in international maritime transport services and protective devices have been increasingly adopted by a large number of developing countries. Among the measures which might be identified as being particularly distortive are: policies of unilateral cargo reservation for the national flag (generally implemented bilaterally by two trading partners who mutually agree on a division of their seaborne trade in the form of a shipping agreement); the creation by LDCs of central freight bureaux (CFB) on the territory of their trading partners (obliging shippers to channel their shipments to and from the country concerned through the latter's CFB, which in turn allocates cargoes to national flag ships); and restrictions on the ability of foreign carriers to invest in facilities such as container terminals or multimodal transport infrastructure. Investment questions may also arise where foreign shipping lines seek, through the establishment of a branch or subsidiary, to operate under another country's flag where that flag has been granted exclusive access to certain specific maritime transport activities. Restrictions on right of establishment and foreign investment have been described as being at the heart of the maritime problems that certain OECD countries are experiencing with key Asian trading partners. Of all the measures undertaken, cargo reservation, touching almost exclusively liner cargo movements, is regarded as the most widespread barrier to trade. For many developing countries, however, full realisation of targeted trade is hindered by two factors: the difficulty of monitoring and enforcing cargo reservation for national ships; and the insufficiency of national tonnage needed to enable developing countries to carry the trade targeted.

The Convention on a Code of Conduct for Liner Conferences is one of the most comprehensive undertakings affecting a single service sector. Drawn up by UNCTAD, at the instigation of the Group of 77, the UN Liner Convention came into operation in October 1983. To date, 68 countries (including nine OECD Member countries) are contracting parties. The Convention deals with relations between liner shipping companies which are members of conferences and with relations between conferences and shippers. In particular, it gives national shipping lines equal rights to participate in the conference trade while third country lines have a right to a "significant share (such as 20 per cent)" -- often referred to as the 40/40/20 formula. The Convention also deals with the ability of conferences to increase freight rates.

In order to seek to prevent the Convention's cargo sharing provisions from distorting relations between industrialised countries and jeopardising the principle of free competition to which they subscribe, the nine Member countries who have acceded to the Convention thus far have done so on the following basis (known as the Brussels Package):

-- The Convention's cargo allocation provisions have been entirely disapplied in intra-EC trades and, subject to reciprocity, in trades between EC and other contracting OECD countries;

74

-- In trades between the nine OECD countries and non-OECD contracting countries, that part of the trade which is allocated to the OECD country shall be open to redistribution to shipping lines of other EC member states and, subject to a reciprocal opportunity to participate in trades serving their own countries, to other OECD countries.

Non-conference lines are not affected by the UN Liner Convention (although some LDCs have interpreted its provisions as embracing the whole liner sector), nor does the Convention concern dry and wet bulk shipping. An increasing number of developing countries are showing signs of extending government control to dry and liquid bulk shipments. Moreover, there is evidence of a significant increase over the last few years in the number of OECD countries' bilateral agreements with non-members incorporating an explicit 40/40/20 cargo sharing formula for all liner trade movements. A number of treaties go even further and cover certain non-liner cargoes and, in a limited number of cases, the totality of trade between the contracting parties. However, with respect to agreements involving EEC countries, through EC Council Regulation No. 4055/86 of 22nd December 1986, EEC member countries are committed to phase out existing cargo-sharing arrangements contained in these agreements or alternatively to adjust these agreements in order to provide, as soon as possible -- or in any event within a time frame not extending beyond the 1st January 1993 -- for free and non-discriminatory access by all EEC countries to the cargo shares allocated to an EEC country under a bilateral treaty.

In the face of a perceived increase in the adoption of protectionist measures by many developing countries, the OECD Council recently adopted a Recommendation on Common Principles of Shipping Policy which, inter alia, provides for coordinated countermeasures against countries restricting the access of OECD Member country shipping lines to their trades. It should be noted that one OECD Member, Australia, while voting in favour of the instrument as a whole, was unable to associate itself with the principles relating to the coordinated adoption of countermeasures.

In sum, maritime transport services have over recent years witnessed the parallel development of both intense competition in certain areas and growing government intervention. The two have been closely interrelated. Government financial and other support for shipping and shipbuilding has, among other factors, contributed to low real freight rates and over-capacity which, in turn, helped to further fuel cargo reservation and other policies designed to expand market shares. Attempts to expand, or preserve, market shares, in their turn, exacerbated overtonnaging by distorting the market and inhibiting accelerated scrapping. The ordering of these elements is not intended to suggest any particular causal link. Developing countries sometimes characterise their cargo reservation policies as a defensive response to market distortion resulting from subsidised shipbuilding over-capacity. As discussed in Part IB of this document, this argument does not appear to be sustainable.

d. Developing Country Concerns

There seems to have been a shift in focus of developing country concerns related to maritime transport services from user towards provider interests. This is reflected in the work of the UNCTAD Committee on Shipping where, in the early years, the dominant interests were the level and structure of freight rates and protection of shippers' interests. From the early 1970s, attention has been directed rather towards developmental issues and the fostering of national fleets. The concerns discussed below will thus reflect both user and producer interests but without drawing a formal, structured distinction between the two; all developing countries have both shipper and shipowner interests and, frequently, the desire to foster a provider capacity in shipping services is in response to perceived user vulnerability.

The first two concerns addressed (safety and national security) have few, if any, specifically LDC aspects and will be discussed only briefly. The remaining concerns (labour issues, balance of payments constraints and industry support), while not being exclusive to developing countries, have a much greater LDC focus.

i) Safety

Three closely interrelated aspects of safety considerations might be distinguished:

-- The danger of discriminatory application of safety standards as between national and foreign flag fleets, damaging the ability of the latter to compete;

-- A corresponding laxity in the enforcement of safety standards for the national fleet (in an attempt to offset possible weaknesses in competitiveness); and

-- Concern that, in the case of open registry fleets, lack of adequate administrative machinery and accountability may preclude effective enforcement of safety standards and protection of crew.

The attitude of individual developing countries will depend on their balance of interests -- whether as labour-senders, as hosts to open registry fleets or as operators of large national fleets. While the application of safety standards bears importantly on the conditions of competition in maritime transport and thus on the basis of trade in shipping services, care will be needed that any consideration of this question is closely linked to the work of the International Maritime Organisation -- the forum in which maritime safety issues are discussed.

ii) Defence and security

Shipping has a <u>direct</u> national security role to play for many countries, as in, for example, the carriage of sensitive defence equipment. An <u>indirect</u> role may also be invoked, where maritime transport acts as an emergency supplement to the naval fleet. This indirect role is, however, less clear. It has been pointed out that policies of protection and support for maritime transport have generally provided little influence over the types of ships put into service and hence have had little influence on their overall military value (108). Nonetheless, the UNCTAD secretariat has observed that "the creation of a national fleet is an important element in attaining and maintaining national independence ... safeguarding supplies for the national economy and population in times of political crisis" (109). Security considerations may be invoked even more readily by developed countries. Exceptions covering security concerns are found in Article 3 of both the Code of Liberalisation of Capital Movements and the Code of Liberalisation of Current Invisible Operations. Moreover, the increasing resort to offshore registries reflects, as well as concern for competitive opportunities, the growing concern of governments that the fleets under their control are approaching the minimum level needed for strategic or security purposes.

Should it be considered necessary for fleet development to reflect national defence and security interests, it is arguable that the costs of such development should be borne by the community at large rather than imposed on a relatively small group -- the users of shipping services.

iii) Labour-related issues

The question of labour migration, and the need for "provider relocation", is seen to be an important consideration in the area of construction and engineering services. In the maritime transport sector the focus is somewhat different in that the main direct beneficiaries of migrant seafarers from developing countries are developed country shipowners. Migrant labour is a key component of the crews of open registries (or flags of convenience) and, increasingly, of offshore registries. One of the reasons for the increased interest in offshore registries, particularly the Norwegian International Register and the fleets of the UK dependent territories, has been the possibility of using non-nationals at pay scales competitive with those of the open registry flags.

The nature of developing country labour-related concerns is highly differentiated, depending on the circumstances of individual countries. For <u>labour-sending</u> developing countries concerns are likely to centre on conditions of employment of migrant sea-board labour. It is suggested that the ability of shipowners to change their sources of labour supply makes it very difficult for the unions or governments of labour-sending countries to improve working conditions (110). (The International Confederation of Free Trade Unions has been strongly critical of the continuance of open registries). Indeed of those OECD countries which permit a substantial element of migrant labour in their fleets, it seems that where cutbacks have taken place they have fallen hardest on non-nationals.

For developing country <u>shipowners</u> labour-related concerns are more likely to reflect the perception that developed country shipping interests derive an "unfair" competitive advantage from the employment of low-cost LDC ship-board labour. This is closely related to the question of possible barriers to entry associated with open registries, to be considered later.

A careful balancing of these two perspectives will be required for those developing countries, such as <u>India</u> and the <u>Philippines</u>, who find themselves both major labour-senders and operators of large national fleets.

iv) Balance of payments constraints

Data deficiencies and complications associated with maritime fraud make accurate balance of payments statistics for shipping extremely difficult to obtain. Nevertheless, some broad observations are possible. As already noted, almost all developing countries have a large balance of payments deficit in shipping services. The overall deficit in the IMF "shipment" category for all LDCs for whom data were available was approximately 8 300 million SDRs in 1985. This compares with deficits of 1 000 million SDRs on "other transportation" (including passenger services and chartering) and 3 500 million SDRs on "other services" (when Saudi Arabia is excluded). Developing countries recorded a surplus on "travel" of 4 300 million SDRs in 1985. Moreover, the shipment deficit estimate is considerably under-stated because of the absence of data for many Middle Eastern countries and because of the practice of chartering, referred to earlier.

The UNCTAD secretariat, noting that freight payments contribute considerably to developing countries' imbalance in invisibles, has concluded that "the only way to remedy this situation is to pursue a consistent policy of import substitution and of export promotion of shipping services" (111). While this proposition is qualified by UNCTAD, in acknowledging that the net effect on the balance of payments will be considerably less than gross foreign exchange savings because of the cost of providing shipping services, there is nevertheless a presumption that the net effect will be favourable. Such a proposition would need careful scrutiny on a case-by-case basis, taking due account of conditions prevailing in the shipping sector. Moreover, a decision to engage in import substitution in shipping services on balance of payments grounds would need to consider alternative sources of import replacement and the <u>relative costs</u> of domestic production in each of the activities considered.

v) Industry support

Developing country shipping policies, while reflecting concerns such as national security, are most commonly invoked in order to support and protect the national flag. Four elements of industry support will be considered: appeals to equity; perceived vulnerability, which it is hoped to avoid; barriers to participation, which it is hoped to surmount; and potential comparative advantage, which, through infant industry support, it is hoped to realise.

Equity: Much of the support for the national flags of developing countries is grounded on the philosophy that the countries that produce or consume a commodity are, by that fact alone, entitled to a significant share in its transport, without regard to their ability to compete on a commercial basis for that transport. While it cannot be denied that there continues to be an imbalance between LDC participation in trade and their carriage of that trade (in the 1970s, LDCs generated some 40 per cent of world seaborne trade while earning less than 5 per cent of the revenue of world shipping) a distinction needs to be drawn between legitimate concerns to increase the competitiveness of developing country fleets and the setting of arbitrary targets of market participation, regardless of commercial viability.

Vulnerability: Concerns for "equity" are motivated, in part, by a perceived vulnerability associated with dependence on imported maritime services. Development of the national flag is thus characterised as "the final means of achieving a countervailing power" (112). Beyond concerns related to the balance of payments, vulnerability is more frequently associated with two issues specific to maritime transport -- freight rates and the adequacy of shipping services.

-- In discussions within UNCTAD, the Group of 77 has expressed concern that the proportions of freight costs to c.i.f. import values are twice as high for developing countries as for developed. This is true but need not be a cause for contention, reflecting, as it does, factors such as distance, mode of transport and the relationship of volume and value. More specifically, it is claimed by UNCTAD that LDC terms of trade are adversely affected by shipping freight rates -- in liner trades, because of unilateral rate-setting procedures and exploitation of monopolistic power and in bulk trades, because of a tendency for developing countries to have to accept f.o.b. terms for their exports. Each of these claims needs to be considered, however, in the context of the prevailing economic environment of shipping services. Unilateral rate-setting notwithstanding, the power of the conference lines has been greatly reduced and freight rates for both liner and bulk cargoes have, until recently, remained depressed for several years, bringing significant benefit to shippers. Furthermore, f.o.b. terms for LDC exports are partly a reflection of the fact that developed country buyers of developing country exports are, in many cases, able to secure more competitive shipping services than those offered by the LDC exporters. A yet more specific concern is that acceptance of f.o.b. terms for exports of bulk commodities entails a risk that ad valorem transport costs rise with the degree of fabrication, providing effective protection to raw material processors and a disincentive to local processing by the developing country exporter. This concern does not appear to have been substantiated. A study of 14 commodity groups in 40 exporting countries showed 27 cases of freight rate escalation against 13 cases where rates declined. Moreover, an UNCTAD study has found that no generally valid conclusions can be drawn with regard to the effect of ocean freight costs on the development of processing activities in developing countries (113);

-- Notwithstanding some reservations about specific freight rate-related arguments, the general proposition that freight costs can influence the demand for exports of individual LDC exporters is entirely valid. To the extent that this frustrates developing country development, there may be scope for: first, a rationalisation of export procedures in order to reduce overall costs of shipping services; and second, co-operation between LDC shippers' organisations at a national, regional or sub-regional level. Moreover, freight rate considerations may warrant closer scrutiny in particular cases. The establishment of the Pacific Forum Line by the Pacific Forum countries is said, by its very presence, to have forced other shipping lines to hold down their freight rates, while the establishment of a shipping subsidiary by Guyana's bauxite exporter Guybau is said to have enabled Guyana to maintain and expand its market for calcined bauxite (114). The experience of Guyana is based on rather special circumstances, however -- the shipping service being on a joint venture basis with predominantly developed country ownership and control;

-- Concerns about the adequacy of shipping services will be closely related to those associated with freight rates. The underlying contention is that national carriers can be expected to maintain a closer link with the particular trading interests of their country than can foreign carriers. This has not been demonstrated.

Barriers to entry: In seeking to avoid vulnerability, as users of maritime services, developing countries have expressed concern at the barriers which they feel constrain their full participation in international shipping. Five such perceived barriers, each raising complex questions going beyond the scope of this paper, will be briefly considered. While grouped generically as "barriers", the features referred to cover a wide range of issues, encompassing both private arrangements and government intervention, as well as inherent economic and technological aspects of maritime transport.

-- In the liner trade, it has been a major developing country grievance that self-regulation through market forces was ineffective because the conference system, with its frequently autocratic approach to shippers, institutionalised barriers to entry and removal of price competition. This grievance has, in part, been addressed by the UN Convention. Under the Convention, a national line always has a right to enter a conference. It might be concluded that under current conditions liner markets are highly contestable, if not perfectly contestable;

-- In the bulk trades, the UNCTAD secretariat suggests that there is a high degree of control by multinational corporations, exercising control through vertically-integrated operations and making it difficult for developing countries to enter the market. Against this, two UNCTAD expert groups have not found evidence of existing barriers established by multinational enterprises. Moreover, as noted earlier, some developing countries have established an important presence in the dry bulk and tanker trades.

-- Developing countries consider <u>open registries</u> (or flags of convenience) to be one of the major impediments to the expansion of their fleets. It is thus argued that tonnage owned in traditional maritime countries but registered under such flags, "by combining the capital resources liberally available from the developed countries with cheap labour and negligible tax liability, unfairly competes with the tonnage of the developing countries" (115). This is of course an area where LDC interests are highly differentiated. The open-registry countries (<u>Antigua</u>, Bahamas, Bermuda, <u>Cayman Islands</u>, <u>Cyprus</u>, <u>Gibraltar</u>, <u>Lebanon</u>, <u>Liberia</u>, <u>Malta</u>, <u>Oman</u>, <u>Panama</u>, <u>St. Vincent</u> and <u>Vanuatu</u>) as well as certain labour-sending countries, such as the <u>Philippines</u>, have strongly resisted efforts to abolish open registries. Moreover, Liberia, supported by Panama and Cyprus, claims that studies carried out do not show how phasing out would ensure a simultaneous development of the merchant fleets of developing countries (116). There have been major attempts in UNCTAD and elsewhere to eliminate the open registry fleets. These have been mainly directed to requirements of a genuine economic link between flag and ship by nationality requirements in manning, management and ownership. Developed countries, while insisting on the importance of improving safety and working conditions by increased transparency and accountability, do not consider that the economic link elements are matters for an international agreement.

-- The impact of more widely diffused technological change and the increasing <u>capital-intensity</u> of maritime transport services have already been referred to. These tendencies are nowhere more evident than in containerisation and multimodal transport where capital requirements have been seen as a "deterrent to developing countries for an equitable participation in liner shipping" -- seriously hampering their ability to take economic advantage of their rights acquired under the UN Liner Convention (117). The use of increasingly sophisticated computerised technology is now a key feature of container shipping and multimodal activities (as well as of cruise shipping within complex tourism infrastructures). Some aspects of the challenge to developing countries arising from multimodal transport are being addressed by the United Nations Convention on International Multimodal Transport. The Convention establishes rules for the carriage of goods by multimodal transport and seeks to stimulate the development of smooth, economic and efficient multimodal transport services. Whether developing country shipping companies will be able to take full advantage of the opportunities presented by multimodal transport raises fundamental questions about their competitive strengths, to be considered below;

-- The last of the perceived barriers to be touched on also leads directly into a discussion of relative competitive capacities. It is suggested, by UNCTAD, that the granting of direct or indirect <u>subsidies</u> to national shipowners -- a course of action pursued primarily, it is said, by developed countries -- keeps the supply of shipping services at an artificially high level and prevents capital movements to other countries that share a comparative advantage in shipping.

Infant industries and comparative advantage: A dynamic concept of comparative advantage is widely invoked by developing countries seeking to foster the national fleet and the anticipated benefits associated with it, in the form of increased foreign exchange earnings, employment creation and enhanced marketing opportunities. It is widely acknowledged, however, that maritime transport services are highly capital-intensive and becoming more so. On this basis, most developing countries could be expected, a priori, to have a comparative disadvantage in this sector.

Shipping costs can be divided into two components (118): international costs (including bunkering, insurance, port charges and repairs) and national costs, the level of which is determined by labour and capital market conditions in the country of registry. As international costs are the same for all vessels of similar type and efficiency, a country's competitiveness is basically determined by relative national costs. A principal element of such costs is the direct wage bill of crew, where most developing countries, with access to low-cost labour, will have competitive strengths. However, as noted earlier, any analysis of the contribution of wage costs to LDC comparative advantage is complicated by labour mobility in maritime transport and by the shortage of skilled personnel in many developing countries. Moreover, capital charges are even more important than labour costs. While comparative advantage is in large measure a function of the relative height of factor costs (together with the external economies derived from the complex interlinkages between shipping, shipbuilding, maritime research, marine insurance and communication services), competitiveness is increasingly associated with the degree of financial or other support offered by governments.

-- In the bulk trades, some members of an UNCTAD Group of Experts expressed the view that the only developing countries which had achieved "success" in dry bulk shipping were those which had adopted unilateral measures (prompting the policy conclusion, not shared by developed countries, that such measures were thus justified);

-- Similarly, in container transport, it is suggested for example that the Taiwanese carrier Evergreen, while having competitively manned and fuel efficient vessels has been able to bid traffic away from established foreign shipping lines, in large measure, because of preferential treatment by the government.

As pointed out for other sectors, the policy choice for individual developing countries will depend on their assessment of priorities and factor endowments. Even broad generalisations about the relative suitability for developing countries of concentration on either liner or bulk shipping need to be approached with care. UNCTAD has suggested (119) that, at least in the early stages, developing countries might seek to concentrate their maritime transport activities on liner shipping, only later diversifying into bulk transport. According to UNCTAD, capital requirements per job directly or indirectly linked to liner shipping are lower than those for bulk shipping (given the greater requirements for shore-based support staff), while skill requirements for management personnel are lower in liner shipping than in bulk shipping. The case for early concentration on liner shipping is by no means established, however:

-- First, technological change is rendering liner transport and its multimodal linkages increasingly capital and scale-intensive;

-- Second, skill requirements in liner and bulk shipping are quite different, but not necessarily higher in one sphere than the other;

-- Finally, just as consideration of labour-intensity is complicated by the circumstances of individual countries so the impact of capital-intensity may need careful assessment on a country-by-country basis. For some developing countries (such as the Republic of Korea and, increasingly, China) which, by virtue of low wage costs, are highly competitive in shipbuilding, the capital component of shipping may in fact be a source of strength.

5. Construction and Engineering Services

a. Introduction

International trade in construction and engineering services reflects a measure of complementarity between the labour-intensive services which are frequently, though not exclusively, offered by developing countries and the more technically advanced services generally offered by developed countries. This situation prompts two major questions (not exclusive to construction and engineering services) each of which overlaps areas beyond the immediate field of "trade":

-- Recognition of the need for the temporary relocation of personnel in the performance of construction and engineering services;

-- Discussion of the transfer of technology to developing countries and of their capacity to absorb such technology.

These two questions are likely to be of central importance in discussion of the service sector, as developing countries seek to focus attention on service activities where they have important areas of competitive strength. A number of developing countries have had considerable success in exporting construction and engineering services to other developing countries. For developing country exporters of construction and engineering services an important element of any trade expansion in this sector would be their wish to emulate in developed country markets some of the success they have realised in intra-developing country trade.

83

b. Sector Profile

It is difficult to define in advance the boundaries of this sector which to a large extent overlaps with the industrial sector and whose organisation varies from one country to another. Particular difficulty is likely to arise in distinguishing those aspects of construction which might be regarded as constituting trade in services and those which do not. While large international contracts, where design and planning are distinguishable from actual construction work, would generally qualify, local house building probably would not. Consistent with earlier studies, the sector will be taken to include all services, from the initial research to the design, construction, maintenance and operation of industrial, agricultural and mining plant, infrastructure and equipment. It will also be taken to include the activities of specialised consultancy firms as well as services associated with the temporary movement of labour, including independent professionals (engineers, architects, geologists, etc.), semi-skilled and unskilled workers (120).

In considering the nature of the sector, with a particular focus on developing country interests, some important characteristics can be identified:

i)   Trade in construction and engineering services has a large cross-border element. Frequently, establishment is neither needed, in order to provide the service, nor sought by the foreign contractor. On some occasions, however, establishment may be required by the host country, together with conditions on local equity participation;

ii) Activity in the sector, particularly in developing countries, is subject to marked fluctuations, resulting from economic cycles, stop-go policies, and lack of long-term investment programmes. Recent years have witnessed a rapid downturn in construction work in the Middle-East as a result of falling oil prices;

iii) The government frequently plays a vital role both as a client, through the public sector, and as a direct supporter of construction and engineering services (121), but with the importance of the public sector as an originator of demand tending to decrease at higher levels of development (122).

Developing countries have an important role as both exporters and importers of construction and engineering services. Trade between developed and developing countries appears to be much more common than that among industrialised countries, reflecting, in part, the complementarity between the relatively advanced technical services offered by developed countries and the low-cost basic services offered, generally, by developing countries.

As exporters of construction and engineering services the position of LDCs has been seen to depend importantly on the availability of low-cost skilled and semi-skilled labour -- a particularly dynamic factor as development progresses, wage levels rise and new sources of labour are tapped (123). In the early 1980s, construction workers from the Philippines, Thailand and Indonesia could multiply their domestic earnings by factors of 3, 5 and 12, respectively, by working in the Middle East.

As importers, developing countries provide the largest and among the most dynamic markets for international construction and engineering services. In 1985, some 86 per cent of overseas design consultancy was conducted in LDCs, with particular buoyancy in Latin America and Asia (124); 75 per cent of foreign billings in construction work was in developing countries, with significant growth in Africa and, again, in Latin America (125).

Construction and engineering activities within developing countries play a vital role in the development process; over 40 per cent of World Bank project assistance goes to construction work. Drawing on the experience of Brazil and Republic of Korea, particular benefits are seen to flow from the export of construction and engineering services, including:

-- Employment creation. This has been particularly important in Brazil as far as skilled labour is concerned, overseas employment opportunities having prevented too great a redundancy of such workers. The total "employment effect" in the Republic of Korea of overseas construction activity was estimated at 514 000 in 1982.

-- Revenue generation. While representing an extreme case, 45 per cent of Korea's oil bill in 1982 was earned from overseas construction.

-- Capital goods sales. While the link between construction and engineering consultancy and possible follow-up exports of capital goods is both an important focus of technical assistance to developing countries (126) and a likely cause of subsidisation of consultancy contracts (127), the experience of Brazil and the Republic of Korea suggests that this linkage is relatively modest.

-- Upgraded labour skills. Korean workers' skills are considered to have increased as a result of the learning by doing process associated with overseas construction activity (128).

Insofar as some export gains will reflect earnings from labour services it will be necessary, as far as practicable, to distinguish remittances or transfers from migrants settled overseas (normally regarded as outside the scope of trade in services) and the earnings of workers whose temporary relocation is necessary to permit the service transaction to take place. This question will be of vital importance to developing countries. In 1980, total labour earnings by India were equivalent to 20 per cent of merchandise exports.

c. Developing Country Concerns

Developing country concerns relating to trade in construction and engineering services stem from their interests as both importers and exporters and bear upon their activities as both the originators and receivers of trade restrictions. It may be useful to summarise the nature of those restrictions. They cover:

-- The variety of subsidy and risk-sharing programmes offered by governments to national firms, whether operating domestically or (as in the case of export subsidies and tied aid) in third country markets;

-- Discriminatory taxes on profits of foreign firms or on imports of goods and services;

-- The widespread practice of giving preference through government procurement to the services of local firms;

-- Restrictions associated with national bidding procedures;

-- Arbitrariness and lack of transparency in selection processes;

-- Technical standards creating onerous requirements for foreign companies;

-- Restrictions associated with licensing;

-- Local equity requirements associated with foreign direct investment.

-- Barriers to trade in goods directly affecting the provision of construction and engineering services;

-- Restrictions associated with the recognition and relocation of labour needed for the performance of construction and engineering services, on occasions amounting to outright prohibition;

-- Currency restrictions on capital transfers and profit repatriation; and

-- Countertrade and financing requirements.

Developing countries as importers

i) Balance of payments concerns

The large scale of many construction and engineering projects gives rise to legitimate balance of payments concerns in developing (and developed) countries, frequently associated with restrictions on capital transfers and profit repatriation.

ii) <u>Consumer protection</u>.

Concerns for health and safety standards make construction and engineering services a heavily regulated service sector. Questions arising relate to the need for such regulations, as far as practicable, to be transparent, non-discriminatory and not disproportionate to the concerns which prompt them.

iii) <u>Development goals</u>.

A widespread developing country concern is to develop the capacity of indigenous construction and engineering services. This is likely to be prompted by three underlying motivations. Firstly, there is recognition of the sector's key role in economic development and a desire to have construction and engineering services matched, as far as possible, to local requirements. Experience suggests that in some cases locally designed projects in LDCs are more likely to exploit labour-intensive technical change while using more local inputs and better exploiting backward linkages (129). Secondly, many developing countries have infant industry type concerns to realise fully (through a learning by doing process) the employment and revenue potential of the sector, while also reducing dependency on foreign construction companies and the perceived restrictive business practices associated with them. The experience of <u>Ghana</u> and <u>Kenya</u> in fostering nascent contractors suggests that such policies can result in immediate cost savings and improved overall performance, while expediting the development of a competitive domestic industry in the long run (130). In <u>India</u> state involvement and support for local construction and engineering services has been seen as having a demonstration effect in spurring development in the private sector. At the same time, infant industry approaches can impose a cost. It has been suggested that in India the strong protection given to local technological efforts has led to large gaps between Indian and world technologies (131). A third developing country motivation for increased self-reliance in construction and engineering services arises from the need to maintain and replenish the extensive basic infrastructure built up during the 1960s and 1970s; a task which will be expensive or extremely difficult to allocate to foreign contractors.

The policy response to these underlying development motivations is likely to involve a spectrum ranging from total self-reliance to wholly imported services. No developing country will resort exclusively to any one approach, the policy mix depending on the complexity of the project in question, the capacity of the individual LDC and the scope for co-operation with foreign partners. It may nevertheless be useful to distinguish three broad areas within the policy range.

i) Some projects, as in basic construction, will be reserved exclusively for local firms (drawing, as necessary, on support from government subsidies, taxation policy, or government procurement and tendering procedures). Several Latin American countries, for example, apply a "Hire National" policy.

ii) A more common situation is likely to be where projects are open to foreign participation but with conditions laid down in respect of requirements to establish (but with minimum local equity), local content and technology transfer. Such conditions will frequently be associated with host country government involvement. Countries as diverse as Singapore and the Andean Pact nations have adopted elements of such an approach.

iii) Complete reliance on overseas construction and engineering services with few, if any, conditions is likely to be reserved for projects whose complexity is beyond the host country's capacity. It can also arise, however, in turnkey operations. An interesting example of this is provided by Algeria (132) where traditional foreign direct investment in manufacturing has been replaced by the purchase of a fee-bearing service by foreign contractors who design and construct the manufacturing plant. While representing an alternative to traditional investment, the adoption of the turnkey approach in Algeria has been found to produce only limited linkage effects to the domestic economy.

What is likely to emerge is the need for a complementary relationship between domestic and foreign construction and engineering services, to optimise the use of local inputs while fully drawing on foreign resources as a vehicle for the transfer of skills and technology.

Developing countries as exporters

There is no clear line between LDC importer- and exporter-related concerns. For example, infant industry motivations will often reflect the wish to establish a viable export capacity and other countries' barriers in areas such as government procurement, taxation and tendering will preoccupy many LDC exporters. Nevertheless, three major areas of concern can be identified which arise, principally, from developing country export activity in construction and engineering services. They relate to the lack of disposable financial resources, the technology lag and issues associated with the movement of labour.

i) Financial resources

A widely expressed concern of developing countries is that they are unable to match the financial packages offered by developed country exporters of construction and engineering services. In recent years the construction sector has accounted for a large, if declining, share of officially supported export credits and subsidies granted by OECD Members (representing some 10 per cent of total credits in 1985 and 3 per cent in 1986). Notwithstanding the major success of Korean firms in this field, it is reported that they have often failed in international bidding because of unattractive financing terms. Similar concerns have been expressed in Brazil, India and Singapore. While these concerns may be allayed to some extent by increased disciplines in the area of export financing, underlying imbalances between developed and developing country financial capacities in this sector will persist. (As a qualification to this overall observation, it should be recalled that the provision of officially supported export credits can provide an important vehicle for technology transfer).

ii) Technology lag

The corollary of developing countries' goal of seeking technology transfer in building up domestic capacity in construction and engineering services is a concern that they lack the expertise to compete for overseas projects requiring high technology or sophisticated management skills. This concern may be compounded in cases where reliance on foreign technology directly limits developing countries' ability to use that technology in overseas ventures because of restrictive clauses by licensors.

iii) Labour issues

For many developing countries, with a comparative advantage in labour-intensive activities, an immediate concern is to have the movement of skilled and unskilled workers recognised as a legitimate component of trade in services. This concern, which has particular relevance for construction and engineering services, is prompted by obstacles raised by host countries to the admission of foreign personnel, whether under general immigration policy or under more specific restrictions or conditions. A key issue in addressing the concern is to determine the extent to which the temporary movement of personnel is essential for the performance of a particular service. For many activities in the field of construction and engineering services it seems that there is a strong "provider-relocation requirement". The "right to establish" might thus be taken to embrace labour mobility. (As noted earlier the competitive benefits derived from low-cost labour are not confined to LDC enterprises. It is not appropriate therefore to regard labour relocation as an exclusively developed/developing country issue) (133).

Beyond this threshold question, many developing countries (and some developed) are faced with two conundrums. First, how to balance the competitive gains derived from low-cost labour in overseas ventures with concerns that such labour is not unfairly exploited. Second, how to balance the gains derived from the earnings and (potential) skills acquired by personnel relocated overseas with concerns about the drain on domestically available skills that such relocation entails.

Some labour-sending countries have introduced institutional arrangements in an attempt to reconcile these various interests. In the Philippines the recruitment of construction workers to supply overseas firms is the domain of Filipino "construction companies", while in Indonesia construction companies act as sub-contractors submitting bids for the supply of all or a portion of the labour needs of a prime contractor. The government of the Republic of Korea creates a form of legal enclave within the countries to which it sends labour. 97 per cent of Korean nationals working overseas are employed by Korean companies, closely supervised by the Ministry of Construction which takes responsibility for workers' salary and employment conditions (134).

The sovereignty of national immigration policies is not in question. This said, problems associated with labour relocation will not be resolved unilaterally and their treatment is likely to be an important issue in the evolution of the conceptual framework for trade in services. A minimum requirement might be agreement on the nature of "provider relocation" that is necessary for the performance of particular services, such as construction and engineering, together with moves towards mutual recognition of the personal qualifications required for such services.

6. Professional Services

a. Introduction

The direct linkage between professional services and questions of public welfare helps explain the high incidence of regulation in all fields. Underlying motivations to shield local industry from foreign competition are also widespread, however, leading to corresponding opportunities for efficiency gains from a process of trade liberalisation. Such gains are most likely to be realised at the level of the firm, where developed countries, overall, may be expected to have a competitive edge. Developing countries, while standing to benefit from such efficiency gains, will also be concerned to exploit their particular strengths as the providers of relatively low-cost individual practitioners. For many LDCs, this will be couched in terms of the need to recognise provider-relocation (labour mobility) as a possible counterpart to capital mobility and investment issues in the Uruguay Round negotiating framework. But it is at the level of the individual practitioner (particularly those who are not highly skilled) that some particularly sensitive problems are likely to arise -- not least, those associated with certification procedures and immigration policy.

b. Sector Profile

While there is no agreed definition of "professional services", the term can be interpreted as covering a broad range of activities, including the "liberal" professions (lawyers, doctors, accountants, architects, etc.), as well as professional services in areas such as engineering, consultancy and advertising.

International trade in professional services can be _transmitted_ at various levels: by the individual practitioner; by international firms specialising in a particular professional activity; as part of the internal operations of multinational enterprises; through team projects in which developed country firms employ developing country professionals; or through international joint ventures, again drawing together developed and developing country expertise. The _form of trade_ can also differ, whether by remote sale (increasingly through telecommunication channels); by movement of the supplier to the consumer or consumer to supplier; or by sale through an agent, associate or other form of permanent representation in the country of the consumer. While the need for some form of commercial presence seems to be a requirement for most, if not all, branches of professional service, the relative importance of different forms of trade differs significantly from one professional activity to another. The provision of accounting services in foreign markets is linked to foreign direct investment to a much greater extent than is the provision of legal services, where cross-border transactions are relatively more common (135). Finally the way in which professional services are _received_ can differ, whether by individual consumers or by business enterprises.

Given the diverse nature of professional services and the transactions they can entail, particular care is needed in distinguishing:

-- the temporary relocation overseas of individual practitioners required for the provision of their services, and the permanent migration of individual practitioners (of major concern to developing countries but normally considered to be beyond the scope of trade in services). In practice this distinction may be difficult to draw; it has been suggested that many Indian professionals who have migrated to the Gulf states experience an "illusion of impermanence" (136);

-- relatively free-standing professional services and those falling within a specific sector which may be the subject of negotiation in its own right, for example, consultancy activities within the construction and engineering sector;

-- arms-length transactions by international firms engaged in professional services and intra-corporate services performed within multinational enterprises.

Each of these aspects will be touched on here although it should be acknowledged that the relevance of different features of professional services will vary according to the context and parties involved. An OECD study of competition policy in professional services, with particular emphasis on the services of doctors and lawyers, observed that "for the most part, only professionals engaged in private practice raise issues with respect to competition policy" (137). For some developing countries the export of medical and legal services by individual practitioners could be of particular interest (including through the movement of the consumer to the practitioner). At the same time it should be noted that these are precisely the areas of professional services excluded from the scope of national treatment under the U.S.-Canada Free Trade Agreement.

With a particular focus on the interests of developing countries, the provision of professional services is seen to have three important interrelated characteristics.

i) Professional business services have a clear international character, with a limited number of key developed country firms operating on a global basis (138):

-- High degrees of market power have been identified in areas of accounting services targeted to multinational enterprise customers, but with a continuing high degree of competition in the expanding market for medium-size corporate customers.

-- A very large share of the world advertising market is held by international advertising firms, with market concentration much more pronounced in developing than in developed country markets. (The top 5 advertising agencies have average market shares of 38.3 per cent in Europe and 36.6 per cent in Canada, compared with 56.3 per cent in Latin America and 58.1 per cent in the Pacific Area.)

-- In both accounting and advertising the initial drive towards internationalisation came from the desire to preserve strong relationships with clients; in accounting as a result of the post-war rise of the multinational corporation, and in advertising, somewhat later, as U.S., European and Japanese advertising firms began operating abroad in the early 1970s. More recently, it is suggested, traditional patterns of defensive international growth have given way to offensive strategies as the providers of professional business services seek to match their growth in traditional markets by developing national practices within LDC markets (139).

ii) The effective provision of professional services often calls for a careful balance of local knowledge and international activity. An intimate knowledge of the languages, customs, regulations and national aspirations of each local market must often be linked to the advantages offered by global operations through economies of scale, uniform quality and the centralised operation of on-line data bases.

iii) The growing diversification of professional services has blurred the distinction between the professions and other activites. This is reflected in the growth of para-professionals (particularly in law and medicine). Liberalisation opportunities may indeed be greater in the area of non-regulated, para-professional services (as with, for example, legal consultants as opposed to lawyers). Diversification is also reflected in a tendency towards cross-fertilisation (as between accounting and management consultancy). The Government of Singapore, observing that the traditional accounting services have reached maturity and offer limited growth potential, has concluded that "new opportunities lie in the development of services complementary to accounting and auditing, e.g. the development and design of information systems, business advisory services and management consultancy services". While the process of diversification has frequently been accompanied by elements of function-accumulation and consolidation (as in the establishment of legal and medical "supermarkets") there have also been elements of increased specialisation as general practitioners have given way to more specialised providers (140).

Although constituting a relatively small proportion of the workforce, professional services have important linkages with economic growth and development. Three dimensions can be distinguished: international activity, receiver benefits and sender benefits.

At the international level, large accounting firms have been instrumental in enabling corporations to shift from domestic to multinational status while international legal services have been closely related to the growing interdependence of the world economy.

The second level of interlinkage, the impact on the domestic receiver, is likely to yield significant direct benefits in the form of professional services that might not otherwise have been available. Construction and engineering services in the Gulf states have been almost entirely dependent on foreign professionals (and semi-skilled workers). International accounting firms are able to contribute to the smooth functioning of host country capital markets, to improve clients' competitiveness and to assist governments in seeking improved project planning. The capacity of developing countries to absorb such services will of course vary, as will the ability to adopt, on a community-wide basis, new approaches to economic activity. It has been observed that the presence of professional and other foreign workers in developing countries can create a social order divided between a consumer-oriented native population and a productivity-oriented foreign population, with the result that economic growth can occur without the local population acquiring the values associated with modern productive life (141).

Benefits to sending countries from the "export" of individual practitioners of professional services will also vary according to levels of development. Studies have shown that the impact of outward migration (which here will be taken as embracing temporary relocation) "will be more favourable to the advancement of developing countries as their economies are stronger, more diversified and more developed, and the impact will be the more adverse the more rigid and underdeveloped their socio-economic system" (142). It might thus be tentatively concluded that those developing countries whose social and educational infrastructure is sufficiently developed to provide a base for the export of professional services would be among those most able to absorb the resulting benefits, whether through income remittances or through the application of enhanced skills as individual practitioners return to their country of origin.

As discussed in Part IB, developing countries have certain competitive strengths in the provision of individual professional services practitioners. More specifically, in certain geographic and sectoral areas providers of professional services from developing countries have been seen to be replacing European expatriates. This needs some qualification. A tendency has been observed in recent years for new patterns of temporary emigration from southern Europe. As traditional destinations have offered diminishing opportunities, there has been a trend for workers from countries such as Italy and Portugal to seek new employment prospects in developing countries. The incidence of the professions in such migration is significantly higher for developing than for developed country destinations. For migrants from Italy, 27 per cent of those destined for developing countries occupy professional positions, compared with only 5 per cent of those temporarily migrating to other European countries (143).

c. The Regulatory Environment

Some of the trade impediments outlined below relate principally to professional service activities at the level of the firm, others will apply more to the activities of individual practitioners. Some will have general application for all service activities, others will have specific application to professional services.

i) Restrictions on the right to practice

-- Limited recognition of foreign credentials and requirements for local qualification are widespread among professional services. Local qualification need not present an insurmountable barrier as long as foreigners are free to qualify. Many countries, however, use the professional certification process to limit the ability of foreigners to practice within their jurisdictions. This was found to be a problem in 21 of 27 countries covered in a survey by international accountants, Arthur Andersen & Company (144). In the legal profession, the most direct obstacle to local bar admission is the requirement of citizenship.

-- Regulations on the nationality of partners, outright prohibition of partnerships between foreign and national firms and requirements for local ownership have been identified as problems in the accounting, advertising and legal professions. In consultancy services, 12 developing countries have been identified as requiring a proportion of nationals to be represented on staff (145).

-- In some cases, a license to operate may be refused or foreign produced services prohibited (as with overseas sourced advertising materials in Argentina, Brazil, Chile, India, the Republic of Korea, Malaysia and Venezuela).

94

-- At the level of the individual practitioner, it is interesting to note that the right to practice in some OECD countries differs among developing countries, as a reflection of cultural and linguistic linkages. Such provisions, however, would not normally be regarded as an impediment to trade.

. In Portugal, the statutory requirement limiting the number of foreign professional in any company does not apply to Brazilian professionals.

. In France, the medical profession is open to EC nationals and doctors from Andorra, Morocco and Tunisia. (In respect of other countries, foreign doctors must have French qualifications or a recognised foreign qualification and their country must have entered into a reciprocal agreement.)

. In the United Kingdom, full registration can be bestowed on overseas doctors who have recognised medical degrees in Hong Kong, Singapore and the West Indies (as well as Australia, New/Zealand and South Africa) (146).

ii) Restrictions on the scope of activity

-- Foreign accounting firms may have difficulty in attaining "audit corporation status", and where such status is attained, they may be disqualified from providing non-audit services such as tax advice and consultancy.

-- In many countries branches of foreign advertising firms are prohibited from obtaining government or government-related advertising contracts.

-- Restrictions on the scope of a legal firm's activities can result from the fragmentation of an Anglo-Saxon lawyer's activities into several other professions.

iii) Restrictions on the use of firm name

-- In many countries foreign-controlled accounting firms, even if locally-owned, are not allowed to use their international firm name. This restriction, which limits the benefits of international recognition and creates administrative complexities, is regarded as one of the most frequent and significant barriers to trade in accounting services. It is also encountered in respect of legal services.

iv) Immigration provisions

-- The impossibility of gaining an entry visa, the difficulties and delays involved, together with restrictions on the issue of residency or work permits are cited as significant impediments to international activity by professional practitioners.

v) Monetary and fiscal conditions

-- Restrictions on the repatriation of fees, royalties and profits are encountered in many sectors, not least in the operations of international accounting and advertising firms. The survey of accounting firms referred to earlier found restrictions on international payments to be the most important impediment to trade. (Of the 15 countries identified, 7 are OECD Members and 8 developing countries.) Some 27 developing countries have been identified as imposing currency or exchange control regulations on the repatriation of funds associated with consultancy services.

-- Discriminatory tax provisions have been cited as affecting the provision of accounting and legal services by foreigners, while subsidies in the competitive bidding process in support of national health care firms has been identified as a major barrier in health care services.

vi) Access to information and telecommunications services

-- Professional and business executives have replaced research libraries as the major users of on-line data bases. Restrictions on transborder data flows and access to computer facilities will be correspondingly costly as an impediment to trade. Restrictions on data transfers in accounting services have been identified in 9 countries (8 of which are LDCs).

vii) Direct intervention

-- Finally, there may be cases where national authorities intervene directly to suppress the performance of professional services (usually on grounds of incompatibility with local political or cultural interests).

It must be stressed that this brief survey of restrictions on professional services is in no sense definitive. A more thorough examination would need to allow for the particular characteristics which distinguish one professional service from another.

-- The extent of restrictions is likely to differ from one sector to another. It is suggested that lawyers suffer less from establishment-related barriers than do accountants as, in general, they have not built up worldwide practices in the manner of accountants.

-- The nature of restrictions is likely to vary within sectors. Barriers in medical services are likely to be significantly reduced if the service is being provided as part of an aid package.

-- The nature of restrictions in any particular sector is also likely to vary over time. In accounting services, after a period when international operations were relatively unfettered, firms are increasingly encountering governmental or professional constraints.

d. Developing Country Concerns

Developing countries as importers

i) Consumer interests

The direct impact of the professions on the health and welfare of the public is widely invoked in all countries in support of regulations governing entry into and operations within professional services. Clearly, not all regulations can be justified as necessary to protect the interests of consumers. Questions arising relate to the need for such regulations, as far as practicable, to be transparent, non-discriminatory and not disproportionate to the concerns which prompt them.

While, overall, the priority attached to consumer protection might be expected to be lower in developing than in developed countries, in some circumstances it may be felt, within LDC's, that specific consumer interests or requirements are more likely to be met by locally provided services. This has not, however, been clearly demonstrated (147).

A further question arising is the extent to which consumer interests can be met through self-regulation. A number of international advertising companies issue guidelines to their subsidiaries overseas to conduct advertising in accordance with the International Code of Advertising Practice. It has been concluded, however, that self-regulation may not always be adequate, especially in controversial areas and that the general trend is towards increasing government regulation of advertising (148).

ii) Cultural integrity

Some professional services are likely to be regulated in order to preserve the cultural integrity of the host nation. As noted earlier, in such cases care will be needed that underlying concerns are not used as a pretext for protectionist policies.

iii) National security and sovereignty

National security and sovereignty concerns are likely to relate to issues both of general, cross-sectoral significance, such as controls on transborder flows of sensitive data, as well as more specific questions such as those arising when foreign lawyers are employed to defend the interests of multinational enterprises engaged in legal action against host governments.

iv) Balance of payments concerns

Restrictions on the repatriation of fees, royalties and profits have been seen as a significant barrier in accounting and consultancy services. Such restrictions are principally motivated by the need to manage foreign exchange and may simply constitute a legitimate temporary delay in remittances occasioned by balance of payments constraints. These restrictions are likely to represent a more deep-seated problem when they are used to circumscribe the relationship of the local entity with the international organisation, or when a sustained balance of payments problem gives the restrictions a long-term nature.

v) Industry support

Many of the measures restricting trade in professional services will reflect an underlying concern to protect local producer interests. Of the barriers outlined above, a number stand out as going beyond the immediate requirements of consumer protection or national security, these include: bans preventing foreigners from obtaining local qualifications; discriminatory licensing; establishment regulations based on nationality; and restrictions on the scope of activity such as denial of access to government purchases.

Some measures may be designed to protect activities other than professional services. For example, controls on transborder data flows may be introduced to shelter local data processing firms from foreign competition. For the most part, however, protective measures will be in direct response to calls for assistance from the professional service sectors and professional associations themselves. The underlying motivations, frequently associated with infant industry-type considerations, will correspond broadly to those identified in other sectors; the desire to realise the benefits of potential comparative advantage more quickly than might otherwise be the case and to reduce the perceived vulnerability associated with dependence on foreign sourced services.

Developing countries as exporters

In the area of professional services, as in other sectors, the distinction between LDC importer and exporter-related concerns will often be blurred. For example, developing country motivations to foster local capacities will reflect not only concern at a perceived vulnerability as importers, but also a wish to establish a viable export capability. Developing country interests as exporters of professional services focus on two principal areas: labour-relocation issues and a perceived relative lack of financial resources.

i) Provider-relocation issues

A threshold question for many developing countries in discussions on a negotiating framework for services in the Uruguay Round is their concern to have the temporary movement of skilled and unskilled workers recognised as a legitimate component of trade in services. This is frequently proposed as a counterpart to recognition of investment questions and the flow of capital.

The attitude of individual developing countries to the export of professional services is likely to encompass a range of sometimes conflicting objectives. Moreover, it would be an oversimplication to present the provider-relocation question in purely developed/developing country terms. Some qualifications are in order.

-- Quite apart from developed country <u>consumer</u> interests, developed country services <u>providers,</u> have a major interest in labour-relocation questions as the employers of low-cost developing country labour (most notably in construction and engineering services, cleaning services and maritime transport).

-- Developing countries while wishing to draw on the competitive gains derived from the supply of relatively low-cost professional services will also be concerned that individual practitioners of such services are treated fairly and reasonably.

-- Finally, developing countries will be concerned to balance, on the one hand, the gains derived from income remittances and (potential) enhanced skills acquired by professionals relocated overseas and, on the other hand, the drain on domestically available skills that such relocation entails.

ii) <u>Financial resources</u>

Where the provision of professional services takes place as part of a tendering process for large-scale projects, it is a widely expressed concern of developing countries that they are unable to match the financial packages offered by developed country exporters. This is, for example, a significant aspect of consultancy services in the construction and engineering sector. This problem is subsumed, however, under the broader question of access to financial resources, and as such, is beyond the immediate scope of this paper.

7. <u>Information, Computer and Communications Services</u>

a. <u>Introduction</u>

A discussion of information, computer and communications (ICC) services raises questions beyond the immediate sphere of trade in ICC services per se. The telecommunications infrastructure is an integral element in the development process and any consideration of LDC concerns in this area must impinge on disabilities which can only in part be addressed in a purely trade context.

The merging of computer and communications technologies has widespread implications. ICC services, and the transborder data flows (TDF) they can entail, are an integral part of international banking, insurance, tourism and construction services. There has been a shift towards a global "information economy" in which both financial markets and the real economy have become increasingly information-intensive. The new products and processes which are emerging have major implications for existing regulatory approaches and economic development in all countries, not least the developing countries. The expansion of ICC services offers a distinct prospect of increased opportunities for trade growth and economic development. ICC services also offer a challenge to developing countries if existing technological disparities are not to widen and if LDC competitive advantages in some ICC sub-sectors and, more broadly, in manufacturing are not to be eroded. It is with respect to ICC services that reference to the developing countries' "dilemma" is most frequently made: the concern that recourse to developed country ICC services, while essential in reaping the benefits of international trade and associated technology, can perpetuate dependence on foreign supply and frustrate the development of indigenous production capacities.

There need not, however, be a stark choice of either trade or development. Certain forms of trade will contribute to the development process. But in pursuing the opportunities of ICC trade expansion, and the ripple effects throughout the economy, due consideration will need to be given to the concerns of countries, developed and developing, to nurture viable local industries, to participate as fully as possible in international networks, and to take full advantage of the opportunities for technology transfer. Care will also be needed in distinguishing between liberalisation, on the one hand, and the preservation of appropriate regulations, on the other, particularly as these bear upon sensitive questions of privacy, cultural integrity, public interest, national security and sovereignty.

An attempt has been made to draw material from as wide a range as possible. In particular, this Chapter draws closely on work done in the OECD Committee for Information, Computer and Communications Policy.

b. Sector Profile

In order to encompass developing country concerns as fully as possible, a broad approach will be taken to the scope of ICC services. Consideration will thus be given to the role of ICC services as activities in their own right, to flows of data accompanying international trade and to intra-corporate flows. For definitional purposes, three principal areas will be covered.

-- Computerised information services: Data collection services which store data in a computer system, organise data bases, distribute data, and organise access to data. Access to data occurs on-line via the telecommunications network.

-- Computer services: Data processing services where the supplier uses his own computer equipment to respond to the processing needs of the client; and software, both packaged and customised. While software packages can entail a service component, because of the way they are commercialised they tend to be considered as intangible goods rather than as a service.

-- Telecommunications services: Services ranging from basic telecommunications (via telephony and telegraphy) to more sophisticated or enhanced services. Two important distinguishing aspects of telecommunications services should be stressed at the outset. First, they are closely linked to the provision of telecommunications infrastructure and equipment -- which provides the basis for almost all ICC services and which will be of particular significance for many LDCs, where such facilities may be lacking or deficient. Second, telecommunications services, unlike the relatively unregulated computer services sector, are highly regulated, not least in developing countries, giving rise to particular sensitivities in a context of trade expansion. The obstacles to competing in the market for telecommunications services stem largely from the monopoly enjoyed in almost all countries by a single state Post, Telegraph and Telephone (PTT) authority.

The rapidly evolving and complex nature of ICC services raises a number of definitional problems or grey areas (149). The convergence of telecommunications and computer technologies has transformed the information service markets. The progressive integration of informatics and telecommunications has stimulated new information services and modified existing ones. The overlap between telecommunications, hardware and software and computer services has reached a point where it is difficult, and in some cases impossible, to distinguish separate markets. In particular, it may be difficult to delineate the point when a 'package' leaves the computer and enters the network and therefore at which point the carriage function of the telecommunications service comes into play, and when the application function of the computer/computerised service function ends. Although computerised information and computer services can be provided with or without network facilities, there is a tendency for them to be provided increasingly via networks. This is the new area of telecommunications network-based services (TNS).

The problem of defining telecommunications network-based services is aggravated by attempts to develop a classification system that meets divergent objectives of suppliers, users and policy-makers. TNS [also referred to in some cases as Value Added Network Services (VANS) or Enhanced Services] include, for example, electronic mail and electronic data interchange. They can be provided via private networks of multinational enterprises for intra-corporate communications; by closed user groups [as in banking through SWIFT (Society for Worldwide Interbank Financial Telecommunications) or in aviation through SITA (Société Internationale de Télécommunications Aéronautiques)]; and via public data networks where individual users can connect their personal computer to telephone lines and obtain information stored in on-line data bases.

International transactions in each of the sub-sectors of ICC services are likely to involve varying elements of cross-border trade, commercial presence and foreign direct investment. From the perspective of developing countries, ICC services can be seen as having two broad characteristics, of strategic importance:

-- The provision of ICC services is inextricably linked to rapidly evolving technological change, emanating from industrialised countries. In the area of hardware, the development of new, low-cost transmission techniques, such as microwave, fibre optic and satellite transmission facilities, and the application of computers for switching and network control are fostering competition and providing a potential for trade expansion;

-- In all branches of ICC services multinational enterprises have an important role both as providers, through arms-length sales, and, most importantly, as users, through intra-corporate transactions. The offshore establishments of multinational enterprises have tended to draw ICC suppliers which have followed their corporate clients overseas, sought new markets or established joint ventures with local interests in response to host country requirements. Frequently, the MNE providers will be from industries outside ICC services. Companies such as Boeing Computer Services and General Electric Information Services, taking advantage of idle computer time, account for 80-90 per cent of sales of data processing services by US overseas affiliates. As users, MNEs play a pre-eminent role. Most international transactions in ICC services are intra-corporate, taking place via MNEs' global computer-communications systems.

The spread of ICC services has fostered a process of internationalisation, creating new opportunities for trade growth. It should be stressed, however, that what may be seen as trade opportunities by some countries may be seen by others as a cause for concern, particularly for those countries not at the forefront of modern technology. Three closely interrelated elements can be identified.

i) Declining entry costs. Entry may be made easier as advances in microelectronics reduce the costs of communications.
The incremental cost of additional ICC services may be relatively low. The effect will differ, however, from country to country. As noted earlier, costs of entry will be lowered if all that is required is simply to "plug in" to the network. But this will not be the case where basic telecommunications infrastructure is inadequate.

ii) Changing forms of trade. ICC services are exerting profound changes on the forms of trade, not only through the introduction of new services (such as computer aided design systems in construction and engineering services) but, more fundamentally, through new processes.

-- The tradeability of many service activities is being increased as information technology assumes greater importance relative to capital and labour inputs. Banking is a clear example. The internationalisation of information technology is permitting a measure of disembodied trade in this and other service sectors.

It has thus been suggested that, increasingly, MNE service production is being structured around flows of information rather than of capital or labour;

-- In manufacturing activity, the shift in the 1970s towards increased inputs of information relative to physical labour and raw materials will increase demand internationally for a range of service providers (such as engineers and computer programmers) (150).

This said, the net effect on the trade opportunities of any particular country may be hard to discern. The impact of shifts in relative factor inputs will depend importantly on each country's factor endowments and competitive strengths. The net impact of growth in one form of service activity may well depend on repercussions on other services (where, for example, teleconferencing substitutes for business travel).

iii) "Externalisation". In seeking the benefits of economies of scale, and to take advantage of the growing availability of standardised products/services on the market, some firms may be induced to cease producing ICC services in-house and instead to purchase them from external specialists. Externalisation may increase the availability of some producer services to small firms (including those in LDCs) who would be unable to support the large bureaucratic structure required for in-house provision. However, the structural implications of ICC services are not easily characterised. While there may be externalisation (or function-shedding) in the provision of specialist ICC services, the use of intra-corporate information flows may, at the same time, promote function-accumulation as, for example, banks expand into travel and insurance services.

The nature of the interlinkages created by ICC services has already been alluded to. Two broad, interrelated dimensions will be considered: the central role played by ICC services in the international trade of all other services and the contribution of ICC services to domestic economic activity and development.

The freedom to move information internationally and to gain access to public telecommunication services are of fundamental importance to all service industries operating internationally. The critical importance of information flows is evident in all of the service sectors considered in this document. The result, it is suggested, has been a shift towards a global "information economy" in which both financial markets and the "real" economy have become increasingly information-intensive (151).

The second dimension of ICC linkages is the role they play in binding together all aspects of domestic economic activity and in contributing to development goals. ICC linkages, with a particular focus on LDCs, can be illustrated with reference to two particular forms of ICC services: basic domestic telecommunications and access to international on-line data bases. Each of these provides a vital engine of growth and an essential element in economic planning.

-- The provision of domestic telecommunications services will have important backward linkages into telecommunications infrastructure and equipment -- the basic prerequisite of most ICC services. For example, investment in telecommunications in Indonesia and in the Philippines in 1979 represented some 2 per cent of GDP and over 9 per cent of gross fixed capital formation. For some developing countries, a significant proportion of telecommunications equipment is produced domestically -- India's principal telecommunications equipment suppliers are state-owned companies (Indian Telephone Industries, Bharat Electronics and Hindustan Cables) (152). Input-output analysis indicates that forward linkage from communications services are strongest towards other service sectors, followed by mining and manufacturing, and then agriculture. Apart from the technical problems associated with input-output data, there is a tendency for this form of analysis to understate the qualitative importance of economic linkages. These can be illustrated drawing on the experience of LDCs in both agriculture and manufacturing. In Sri Lanka, the recent introduction of telephone services into several rural towns has enabled small farmers to obtain direct information on capital city prices for farm produce and so demand, and obtain, higher returns for their output. The availability of telecommunications services has been identified as the primary reason for more rapid progress with industrial projects within certain areas of the Maharashtra State of India.

-- The role of basic domestic telecommunications facilities in economic activity is mirrored at the international level by the TDF associated with the on-line data-base market. Such data flows provide a critical element in economic planning. For example, the availability of data bases on the prices of products on world markets increases the transparency of commodity markets and their speed of response to changing circumstances. The use of high speed data networks to monitor developments on world financial markets can increase financial market efficiency by, for example, reducing lags between falling forward prices of foreign exchange and capital outflows. Enhanced market response has become of increased importance as the relative stability and predictability of the major international economic variables during the 1950s and 1960s has given way to a less certain environment (153).

Comprehensive and reliable data on the role of developing countries as providers and users of ICC services are not readily available. The following is intended to provide an impression of this role for each of the ICC branches identified earlier.

i) <u>On-line Data Bases</u> (computerised information services).

-- The U.S. and Canada account for some two-thirds of the total number of <u>vendors</u> of internationally accessible on-line data bases (the largest of the corporations being DIALOG Information Services Inc. and Data Resources Inc. of the U.S. and IP Sharp of Canada). As noted in Part IB of this paper, the role of LDCs is, as yet, relatively modest.

-- As <u>users</u> of on-line data bases, LDCs play a somewhat more active, although highly differentiated role. Nodes of international networks exist in a number of developing countries including <u>Brazil</u>, <u>Chile</u>, <u>Hong Kong</u>, <u>Mexico</u> and the <u>Philippines</u>. Intercontinental leased circuits have been established that offer access to network nodes in such countries as the <u>Ivory Coast</u> and <u>Morocco</u>. It has in fact been suggested, on the experience of <u>Mexico</u>, that the monetary costs of gaining access to on-line information services are within the capability of most countries, both for the necessary investment in equipment (some US$50 000 for a small node and several terminals) and for operational expenditure. This is not, however, a widely held view. The United Nations Centre on Transnational Corporations (UNCTC) comments that new entrants face very high, albeit falling, costs of entry. In many parts of the world there are no international network nodes and the use of intercontinental leased circuits may be prohibitively expensive. <u>India</u>, after several experiments with new techniques of acquiring global data still does not have a fully effective, operational system (154).

-- The net result, in present circumstances, is that while aggregate economic and financial data are widely available on-line for developed countries, the amount of data for developing countries is more limited. The principal producers, transmitters and consumers of on-line data are institutions in developed countries, among which MNEs play a prominent role. The situation in the on-line data base market is, of course, closely linked to the carriage function of telecommunications services which will be considered below.

ii) <u>Data processing and input</u>

As noted earlier, the labour-intensive nature of data processing and input offers opportunities to a number of developing countries, particularly in the form of activities comparable to the offshore processing of manufactured goods.

iii) <u>Software</u>

OECD countries accounted for some 97 per cent of the international software market in 1984. Nevertheless, activity in developing country markets is increasing. Developing country opportunities in software services will be particularly important as these are seen as the driving force within computer services.

iv) Telecommunications services.

-- In the area of basic telecommunications there is a significant
gap between the facilities available in developed and developing
countries. OECD countries account for approximately 79 per cent
of the world stock of telephones and 78 per cent of world main
lines. Telephone density (telephones per 100 people) in 1984,
ranged from 28.6 in North and Central America and 20.43 in
Europe, to 5.02 in South America, 3.34 in Asia and 0.91 in Africa.

-- Telecommunications infrastructure is essential for the provision
of international telecommunications network-based services (TNS),
such as access to on-line data bases. The only international
networks (at the time of writing) are TYMNET, TELENET and UNINET,
which are privately owned by U.S. corporations. Almost
four-fifths of all data-base operations use TYMNET or TELENET.
In the area of closed user groups, developing countries have
become progressively more integrated into the networks. The
initial (1973) membership of SWIFT of 239 banks in 15 countries
has grown to 1 300 banks in 60 countries. SITA now encompasses
over 240 airlines. A new computer reservation system (ABACUS) is
being introduced by Cathay Pacific of Hong Kong, Singapore
Airlines and Thai International.

-- The provision of telecommunications services in many LDCs is
evolving rapidly, making broad characterisation difficult. For
some countries, such as the African LDCs, the immediate and
pressing need for improved telecommunications services may be met
(and perhaps most effectively met) by relatively unsophisticated,
analogue structures. Other developing countries, such as Brazil
and Saudi Arabia already have relatively sophisticated systems.
Looking further ahead, it has been suggested that by the
year 2000 most countries of East Asia will have reached what is
now regarded as the most advanced stage of telecommunications
services -- using fibre optic and satellite transmission and
completely digitalised switching. An important element in the
evolution of developing countries' telecommunications services
will be their access to, and direct participation in, satellite
facilities. While the LDC experience is again highly
differentiated, areas of significant progress are evident
-- India's multi-function Insat satellite has made a major
contribution to telecommunications across the country, while
China is now offering its own satellite service to other
countries.

-- Recent developments in the Caribbean provide an interesting
illustration of the central role which the carriage function of
telecommunications services plays in drawing together other
elements of ICC services. A joint venture (involving the
Jamaican Government and companies from the U.S. and Japan) is to
establish a high speed telecommunications (teleport) facility in
Jamaica, largely in response to the opportunities presented by

the Caribbean data-processing industry, based as it is on low production costs and proximity to a major developed country market. This situation may not, however, be replicable in other LDC regions and even where it is questions may still arise about the need to develop indigenous (as opposed to imported) technologies in ICC services and about the prospect of moving from labour-intensive ICC activities into more complex, skill-intensive fields. These are among the range of concerns that will face LDCs as they seek to maximise the development impact of the information economy.

c. The Regulatory Environment

At the national level, changes in OECD countries' regulatory frameworks have, on the whole, been aimed at liberalising service provision. These changes have also affected the administrative provisions for telecommunications. For example, one of the prerequisites to ensure fair and equal treatment is neutrality in the formulation, application, and interpretation of regulations. This implies separation between operational activities of telecommunication administrations and regulatory activities. There is a clear trend toward separating regulatory from operational functions in telecommunications in OECD countries. In general in developing countries there is no separate regulatory function.

At the international level, the exchange of telecommunication services between two or more telecommunication administrations has been undertaken within the framework of the International Telecommunication Convention (ITC), its Regulations, and the Recommendations of the International Telegraph and Telephone Consultative Committee (CCITT) of the International Telecommunication Union (ITU). While ITC Regulations provide the broad regulatory framework, CCITT Recommendations, which are not binding, provide the operational details. It is important to recognise that the existing framework is still broadly based on the traditional view, which was widely accepted throughout OECD countries, that telecommunication services were best offered on a monopoly basis because of arguments related to the economic characteristics of telecommunication services and socio-political and equity concerns.

-- The ITC Regulations have over the last few years been under review by the Preparatory Committee of the World Administrative Telegraph and Telephone Conference (PC-WATTC) which had a mandate "to consider proposals for a new regulatory framework to cater for the new situation in the field of new telecommunication services". The WATTC which met at the end of 1988 agreed on a new set of Regulations which place emphasis on national sovereignty and the right of ITU members to grant or withold authorisation for telecommunications services within their own territories. The Regulations also allow for special arrangements to be made between member states.

-- Many CCITT Recommendations have been aimed traditionally at constraining competition. For example, for tariffication purposes it is recommended that "the rates adopted should be such as to avoid harmful competition among different types of services". In the past, there has been a tendency by countries to adhere to these Recommendations at least insofar as relates to international telecommunications services. However, recent initiatives by several OECD countries and ongoing negotiations, which are aimed at opening up the international provision of value-added network services, are not compatible with existing Recommendations.

d. Developing Country Concerns

Before considering developing country concerns in the area of ICC services it may be useful to recall briefly the nature of the impediments to trade with which these concerns are frequently associated. Some of this discussion will of necessity touch on aspects of the regulatory environment, referred to above.

At the outset it should be acknowledged that the notion of impediments to trade in ICC services is capable of quite distinct, but equally valid, interpretations. This is clearly demonstrated in the case of on-line data bases.

-- For some interested parties, such as multinational providers of data base information, concern will be that telecommunications tariff charges and other policies in potential markets act as a barrier to trade by discouraging domestic users from accessing foreign on-line ICC service providers;

-- For others, such as potential LDC users of international data, the concern may be rather that telecommunications infrastructure costs and lack of training and education act as a handicap to the use of on-line data bases.

This differing perception is not a simple "North-South" issue but it does bear importantly on the emphasis which developing countries will place on any trade expansion process; it is perhaps what prompted a developing country commentator to call for a distinction between access to markets on the one hand, and access to resources on the other. From a trade policy perspective it will be important to distinguish between barriers, which result from government policy and which prevent or distort trade, and handicaps, which result from the inherent insufficiency of many developing countries' educational and technical environment and which impede their participation in ICC activities.

Many countries have adopted some form of official "informatics policy". It will be recalled that measures affecting trade in ICC services (applied in developed and developing countries alike) encompass the following:

-- Direct discouragement of transborder data flows (in and out of the country) by regulatory or taxation policies, including the requirement that data bases be stored domestically;

-- Restrictions by government owned or controlled PTTs, on the use of private leased line capacity and the ability to provide enhanced services to third parties, as well as prohibitive or discriminatory charging for dedicated leased lines;

-- Lack of internationally agreed standards and discriminatory application of controls on the type of equipment acceptable for interfacing with the domestic communications system;

-- Restrictions on the use of computer facilities in foreign countries for data processing or information retrieval;

-- Use by foreign PTTs of monopoly power, including the "whipsaw" effect where the PTT monopoly seeks to play-off competing service suppliers from another country one against the other in order to obtain favourable terms. (Such a practice, it should be noted, is of concern to developed rather than developing countries);

-- Foreign equity restrictions or joint venture requirements in domestic ICC service industries;

-- Lack of transparency and due process in the implementation of regulations;

-- Restrictions associated with government procurement policies.

Any assessment of the importance of developing country concerns in ICC services is complicated by the blurred boundaries of activities within the sector and by the diversity of countries and interests involved. Concerns will differ: from one country to another (depending, for example, on the stage of development, on differing value systems and on the adequacy of the communications infrastructure); from one branch of ICC activity to another within individual countries; and from one interest group to another within a single branch of activity within individual countries (for example as between domestic users and domestic providers of on-line data base information). In this, as in all other sectors examined, none of the concerns identified is unique to developing countries

i) Consumer service and revenue considerations

In many countries, but particularly in the poorer developing countries, rural hinterlands are very thinly served with basic telecommunications.

-- In Papua New Guinea, for example, there is an efficient telecommunications system for those with interests overseas and in the eight main cities. But 85 per cent of the population, located in outlying villages, is bereft of any modern communications.

It is sometimes suggested that if such countries become subject to the same pressures for more competitive telecommunications services that have become evident in developed countries, their rural areas are likely to continue to have only a very rudimentary telephone service. The argument is linked to that which sees the provision of a basic telecommunications network as a natural monopoly; where the size and long-term nature of the investment in communications infrastructure and the need to provide an adequate public service, even in uneconomic parts of the market, calls for a public or private (regulated) monopoly. This is not to suggest, however, that the private sector may not be able to build up efficiently the domestic telecommunications structure of particular developing countries.

Concerns related to the provision of a universal service and a perceived need to maximise revenue opportunities may have important implications for user charges. Developing country PTT administrations may have only a limited interest in leasing private lines at flat rates to large users. Rather, they may seek to charge at a rate which is sensitive to volume, thus entailing a considerable cost increase for multinational users.

Discussion within OECD has identified the need to consider the policy options available to balance social policy and equity objectives with efficiency in production of telecommunications services (155).

ii) Privacy

Concerns over data protection and privacy first brought transborder data flows to the forefront of international attention. Starting in the early 1970s, a number of European countries adopted data-protection laws to safeguard the privacy of their citizens and, in some cases, their corporations.

At the time, these regulations were viewed by multinational enterprises with some concern -- as a potential source of arbitrary and discriminatory treatment and as a barrier to the storage and movement of internal data files. In practice, the adaptation of computerised management systems has facilitated compliance with these requirements without undue difficulty or expense, and the need for regulations to safeguard privacy is not seriously questioned.

iii) Intellectual property rights (IPRs)

It is recognised that the interests of the owner of a technology may often be at odds with those of parties wishing to acquire that technology. Creative activity needs to be encouraged and, as necessary, protected. At the same time, however, exclusive IPRs, although limited over time, entail an anti-competitive element which may lead to abuses of dominant position: as when innovations are made available only at excessive prices. The maintenance of IPRs in a situation where the holder refuses to work his innovation can effectively deny development opportunities to potential users and has prompted compulsory licensing of innovations in some countries. While this is not a "North-South" issue (a growing number of more advanced LDCs will be concerned to protect their IPRs), many developing countries will be the acquiring party and this question may be seen, by them, as falling within the broad ambit of "access to resources". Beyond the question of differing perceptions of IPRs, many countries, and particularly poorer LDCs, may be faced with practical constraints arising from the administrative costs of ensuring that intellectual property rights are protected. Against this background, two particular problems arise in an ICC services context:

-- First, where restrictions are imposed on the import of ICC services, preventing local companies from making legitimate products available, pirates often fill the gap. In this situation, restrictions on market access create an environment in which intellectual property rights will be infringed. Where import barriers are particularly high, even improved intellectual property protection may have only marginal effects. This is the case in the Brazilian software market.

-- Second, rapid technological change may create a situation in which some ICC services find themselves in a "regulatory vacuum", falling outside existing intellectual property systems. It is suggested that neither patents (covering inventions) nor copyrights (covering writings) fit well the case of software. Again the distinction between packaged and custom software is important. In principle, packaged software is covered by copyright provisions.

Breaches of IPR can be extremely costly. It is estimated that in 1984, losses from piracy of U.S. copyrighted software in nine LDCs (Brazil, Egypt, Indonesia, Republic of Korea, Malaysia, the Philippines, Singapore, Taiwan and Thailand) amounted to some US$128 million for domestic markets only (156). It should be noted, however, that accurate cost estimates are difficult to obtain (for example, in comparing the relationship between the actual consumption of pirate software and the consumption of legitimate software that would have occurred in the absence of piracy).

Some measure of adaptation may provide partial relief from IPR breaches. Apple Computers, for example, has sought protection from imitators by incorporating its proprietary software into a custom chip in order to benefit from patent laws. More far-reaching proposals envisage the establishment of minimum legal standards of regulation for ICC services reconciling intellectual property laws or substitutes for them in the form of know-how contracts. Pending any such arrangements (and, most importantly, effective means of enforcing them), bilateral approaches may offer some scope for relief, while also raising questions about multilateral application and third-country effects. It is understood that in 1986 discussions between the United States and the Republic of Korea enabled the U.S. to obtain protection for five years in the case of computer software. Doubts have been expressed, however, within the United States' legal community, about the effectiveness of this bilateral arrangement (157). The agreement with the Republic of Korea, which covers published program works created after 15th July 1987, is said to have two shortcomings. First, the exclusion of unpublished works from protection could make the United States' most sensitive software (such as computer-aided engineering, usually protected as trade secrets) vulnerable if they were to be "published" in the Republic of Korea. Second, the absence of a transition period leading up to July 1987 would enable Korean defendants to argue in almost all cases that a U.S. computer programme was not entitled to protection because it was a copy of a work created prior to 16th July 1987.

iv) Cultural integrity

Developing country concerns about cultural identity are clearly reflected in the proceedings of the Conference on African Informatics Integration (Abidjan, November 1979) where it was recommended that external cultural information disseminated by mass-media be screened "in order to protect populations from unconscious cultural alienation". Developed countries too have expressed a pervasive concern about cultural and societal integrity. The difficulty will be in ensuring that such concerns are not used as a pretext for the protection of domestic commercial interests.

v) Public interest, national security and sovereignty

These closely interrelated considerations reflect a general concern, in both developed and developing countries, that as the international economy becomes more information-intensive and inter-linked, some measure of national control is lost. The need to preserve national security and sovereignty was a recurring theme of the Third Conference of Latin American Informatics Authorities (Buenos Aires, October 1979).

A number of specific concerns have been identified.

-- Where data important to the functioning of the economy are stored overseas a risk is entailed that access will be cut off for international legal, technical or political reasons. (Brazil's earliest controls on data transfers in 1978 were, in part, prompted by concerns that a planned nuclear power plant had its computerised data base overseas);

-- Government may perceive a need to stem the flow of certain types of sensitive information to selected countries or regions;

-- Some developing countries have opposed the use of satellite remote sensing systems or other advanced detection techniques which could provide foreign interests with better data on natural resource availability than is available to local authorities. Brazil and seven other South American countries have taken advantage of the lack of any international definition of "space" to claim rights of sovereignty extending to satellites and other "space objects";

-- Concern has been expressed in African countries that, because of deficiencies in basic infrastructure, communications between them are often transmitted through countries which are geographically located outside the African continent. (This is, of course, only one of many concerns arising from the lack of an adequate national communications infrastructure in many developing countries).

A case widely referred to by LDCs, and which illustrates one aspect of concerns related to access to data, involved Dresser-France, the French subsidiary of a U.S. multinational. It is reported that in order to enforce sanctions prohibiting the supply to the Soviet Union of pipeline-related equipment by foreign subsidiaries of U.S. companies, the U.S. Head Office was required to cut all technical communications with its French subsidiary. It can be argued, however, that here the question of access to TDF was subsumed under the broader question of the extraterritorial extension of national jurisdiction and that discussion is most appropriate in that context.

In any examination of concerns relating to national security and sovereignty it will be necessary to draw a distinction between those concerns warranting appropriate regulation, those best addressed by developing local capacities in data collection and those most appropriately addressed in the context of extraterritoriality.

vi) Balance of payments constraints

In each of the previous sectors in which LDC concerns have been examined balance of payments concerns have been a significant factor. ICC services are no exception, although comprehensive data are lacking. Developing countries identified as imposing foreign exchange restrictions, notably on the payment of licence fees for computer services, include Brazil, the Ivory Coast and Nigeria. Restrictions on the transfer of funds have been applied in Malaysia.

vii) Infant industry support

Many of the measures applied in the area of ICC services are intended, if not explicitly, to support nascent domestic industries. Moreover, while many of the concerns referred to so far have a particular focus on one branch within ICC activities, infant industry concerns arise across-the-board (although for individual countries, often with selective application).

The basic objective of infant industry support is to apply a learning-by-doing process. Through this, it is hoped that the realisation of potential comparative advantage and a measure of self-sufficiency in ICC services will be attained more quickly than would otherwise be the case. Brazil's informatics policy, which is perhaps the most comprehensive example of the infant industry approach in ICC services, seeks to maximise the amount of information resources (computers, software, data bases and skills) located in the country, together with some degree of technological and operational autonomy of local affiliates of multinational enterprises (158). It is implicit in such an approach that it may be necessary to forgo some immediate benefits associated with the import of ICC services in order to foster longer term development goals. The corollary of this argument is the concern that liberalisation of ICC services would block the possibilities for developing countries to develop their own domestic data services and informatics industry in accordance with their national policy objectives.

Three underlying motivations for the development of such national capacities can be identified.

-- To reap the direct economic benefits of participation in a fast growing area of activity;

-- To obtain ICC services most suited to local requirements. This arises, in part, from apprehension about the role of multinational enterprises as, simultaneously, both data equipment suppliers and data service providers, and pressures which may arise for standards to conform to the technical configuration of the existing hardware and software they market. It has been suggested that little of the telecommunications research and development in industrialised countries has been directed to the distinctive needs of developing countries -- such as for more cost-effective equipment in remote areas (159);

-- To reduce the disabilities and perceived vulnerability faced by developing countries in this sector.

Developing country disabilities in ICC services, whether through inadequate infrastructure or lack of skilled personnel, are clearly evident and have been a recurring element of this note.

It is widely perceived in developing countries that these disabilities bring with them significant vulnerability, not only putting at risk national sovereignty and public interest (as earlier considered) but also undermining the basis of developing countries' competitive strengths and their indigenous industrial development. These latter concerns warrant further attention. They derive from two principal fears: first, that information technology has a negative impact on the importance of labour costs as a competitive advantage (by increasing the information component of the production process relative to the labour and material components); and second, that ICC services provide the basis for the centralisation of corporate decision-making functions, enabling multinational enterprises to manage affiliates in developing countries with minimal transfer of technical skills and information, thus heightening LDC dependence (160). These concerns need to be balanced by the opportunities presented by ICC services and by the fact that MNE centralisation policies of the 1970s may have given way to more flexible approaches. "Centralisation" concerns nevertheless contribute to the underlying motivations for the development of indigenous ICC skills and capacities.

Infant industry support has been invoked, variously, by developing countries in respect of all aspects of ICC services and related production activities.

-- Computer hardware. Foreign processing can threaten the development of domestic computer hardware manufacture. If real-time transborder processing can be performed cheaply then computer/computerised services can be obtained overseas (through TDF) at substantial savings, thus reducing, inter alia, the demand for locally produced computer hardware. The initial rationale for Brazil's control on TDF was to protect domestic computer manufacturers. TDF controls together with the "market reserve" policy (giving Brazilian firms exclusive rights to manufacture and sell products within designated categories) have seen domestic sales of computers and peripherals grow from $800 million in 1978 to $4 billion today.

-- On-line data bases (computerised information services). Support for local data bases has also been considered worthy of attention on infant industry grounds. Again, this has been the approach adopted by Brazil, where commercial access to international data bases has been relatively restricted on the grounds that they did not involve the development of local data base capacities. Petitions by Reuters to provide quotation services in Brazil were systematically delayed until the network of CMA Engenharia de Sistemas was in place (161).

-- Computer services. As noted earlier, infant industry-type support of software and processing services has been identified in a number of developing (and developed) countries. India's position as a major exporter of software is due, in part, to government policy permitting imports of computer equipment if the importer undertakes to export its software. (100 per cent of the output of a recent Texas Instruments' Indian joint venture will be exported). A number of LDCs including the Republic of Korea, several other Asian countries, as well as Mexico, are reported to be preparing domestic legislation aimed at protecting, or further protecting, software production. For many developing countries, indigenous software production may be considered a more promising avenue for infant industry support than hardware production in that it does not require large capital investment or extensive physical infrastructure. Moreover, it is suggested that the special informatics requirements of LDCs (often deriving from the importance of the rural sector) may render inappropriate the simple transplanting of developed country software applications (162).

-- Telecommunications services. Support for the provision of basic telecommunications is likely to be advocated on the basis of "universal service" arguments. Even here, however, infant industry considerations may also be invoked in resisting the admission of foreign suppliers.

It has been suggested that, in the case of Brazil, the range of support measures applied to domestic ICC services has been successful in increasing the amount of domestic information resources, particularly in terms of local production capacities, technology and skilled human resources. At the same time, it is said, national control over the ICC sector has increased and

115

general access to information has improved (163). This is not to say, however, that Brazil's experience is necessarily a valid model for other LDCs, nor that such an approach can be adopted without a cost.

In considering LDC concerns, reference frequently is made to the dilemma facing developing countries in the area of ICC services -- taking advantage of imports, while essential in reaping the benefits of internationally traded services and associated technology, can perpetuate dependence on foreign supply and frustrate the development of an indigenous production capacity. Put differently, this can also be seen, in part, as a question of balancing the respective interests of domestic ICC users, on the one hand, and domestic ICC producers, on the other. This tension may be reflected at the bureaucratic level within national administrations. The implementation of Brazil's policy on informatics has entailed longstanding difficulties between the Special Secretariat of Informatics (SEI), concerned, principally, with developing domestic computer hardware production, and the Ministry of Communications (MINICOM), concerned with exporting communications and improving access to outside data bases. (The conflicting priorities of SEI and MINICOM even led to differing approaches in defining a "national" firm, with SEI applying much more rigorous criteria) (164).

In fact, the LDC dilemma, although a genuine preoccupation, need not involve a stark choice of either trade or development. As seen earlier, a trade liberalisation process can indeed contribute to the development goals of developing countries, by improving the efficiency of resource allocation and by encouraging the transfer of necessary skills and technology.

e. Scope for Regional Cooperation

The process of liberalisation may need to make specific allowance for the goals of regional co-operation and integration. In the ICC sector this might apply particularly in the areas of shared data resources and access to regional public networks. It has been suggested that between a national information system and the international market, some interface at the regional level may be desirable for developing countries, leading to the establishment of regional data networks, analogous to EURONET. The establishment of regional networks (with the United Nations regional commissions or regional development banks as possible focal points) may be the most effective way for many developing countries to overcome underlying economic disabilities and to benefit from economies of scale in gaining access to international on-line data bases. More specifically:

-- The Intergovernmental Bureau for Informatics (33 out of 36 member countries being LDCs) has been active in promoting discussion of guidelines for transborder data flows in regional conferences of developing countries;

-- SELA Decision No. 221 on Modalities of co-operation in the field of Informatics and Electronics, provides for information sharing and initiatives to buttress regional self-sufficiency.

Regional co-operation has also proved effective in the sharing of satellite facilities in, for example, the Middle-East (through the Arab Satellite Communications Organisation whose two-satellite system was launched in 1984), and in the zone around Indonesia (through Indonesia's Palapa satellite system). Finally, regional co-operation -- such as that embodied in the ABACUS computer reservation system -- has enabled LDCs to scale barriers to market entry that might otherwise have been insurmountable to individual developing countries.

NOTES AND REFERENCES

1. The extensive forward linkages from individual service activities, with perhaps relatively limited opportunities for economies of scale, towards manufacturing and primary industry with greater opportunities may, in certain cases, imply high general equilibrium costs of protection. Data deficiencies, however, are likely to preclude any accurate measurement of this observation. The combination of rapid internationalisation of many service activities together with growing areas of skill-intensity also suggests major potential gains over the longer-term from the skills transfer frequently associated with establishment-based trade in services.

2. It may in fact be considered necessary to establish priority as between producer and user interests. In a study prepared for the Royal Bank of Canada, analysing proposals for a Canada/US agreement on traded computer services, it was assumed that, for Canada, the interests of users of computer services overrode the interests of providers of computer services, and that the interests of both overrode the interests of manufacturers of computer hardware. See R de C Grey, Traded Computer Services, Ottawa, 1983.

    Because of the widespread importance of "producer services" and the fact that service users frequently are not final consumers but rather producers (and exporters) of other services or goods, import protection of relatively labour-intensive services may involve a direct burden on exports in addition to the burden, identified in goods trade analysis, which is "shifted" to exporters through upward adjustments in the wage rate. For discussion in the goods context see K.W. Clements and L.A. Sjaastad, How Protection Taxes Exporters, Trade Policy Research Centre, London, 1984.

3. United Nations Centre on Transnational Corporations, "Role of Transnational Corporations in Services, Including Transborder Data Flows", E/C.10/1989/14, 17 February 1989.

4. Larry E. Westphal, "Empirical Justification for Infant Industry Protection," World Bank Staff Working Paper, No. 445, 1981. For a further discussion of the relative economic efficiency of alternative forms of service sector protection, see Brian Hindley "Service Sector Protection: Considerations for Developing Countries", The World Bank Economic Review, Vol. 2, N°. 2, May 1988. A theoretical discussion of

subsidies for education and training is contained in James R. Markusen, "Trade in Producer Services: Issues Involving Agglomeration Economies, Human Capital and Public Inputs", Institute for Research on Public Policy, mimeo, Ottawa, December 1986.

5.   The need for such cooperative efforts in meeting user needs is evidenced by the problems encountered by US banking and insurance firms establishing operations in the recently liberalised market of the Republic of Korea. See Financial Times, 23 November 1988.

6.   A study of the two main exports of Fiji, sugar and tourism, indicated that 53 per cent of tourist expenditure was on imported inputs compared with only 14 per cent of receipts from sales of sugar. See Edward Dommen, Invisible Exports from Islands, UNCTAD Discussion Paper, No. 9.

7.   OECD work (subject to continuous updating and revision) on the development of a conceptual framework for trade in services is contained in OECD "Elements of a Conceptual Framework for Trade in Services" 1987.

8.   For further discussion see D. Germidis and C-A Michalet, International Banks and Financial Markets in Developing Countries, OECD, 1984; S.K. Modwel, K.N. Mehrotra and S. Kumar, Trade in Services, Indian Institute of Foreign Trade, November 1984; R.M. Pecchioli, The Internationalisation of Banking: The Policy Issues, OECD, 1983. A discussion of the nature of comparative advantage in banking and financial services is contained in Thierry Noyelle, New York's Financial Markets, Westview Press 1989.

9.   See, for example, U.S. Department of the Treasury, Report to the Congress on Foreign Government Treatment of United States Commercial Banking Organisations, 1979 (and subsequent revisions).

10. Kazumasa Iwata, "Liberalisation of Trade in Financial Services," mimeo, January 1987. Paper prepared for 16th PAFTAD Conference. Wellington, New Zealand. January 1987.

11. Alan Gelb, "Liberalizing Banking and Financial Services: Costs and Benefits for Developing Countries", mimeo, May 1988. Paper prepared for Seminar of Centre for Applied Studies in International Negotiations. Geneva. May 1988.

12. Paul de Grauwe, "The Micro and Macro Economics of Financial Deregulation: A Survey," mimeo, July 1987 Paper prepared for World Bank conference "Developing Countries' Interests and International Transactions in Services" Washington. July 1987; and World Bank, World Development Report, 1987.

13. André Sapir and Ernst Lutz, "Trade in Services: Economic Determinants and Development-Related Issues," World Bank Staff Working Paper No. 480, 1981.

14. UNCTAD, "Insurance in developing countries: developments in 1984-85," TD/B/C.3/222, February 1987.

15. UNCTAD, "Insurance in the context of services and the development process," TD/B/1014, August 1984.

16. Brian Hindley, <u>Economic Analysis and Insurance Policy in the Third World</u>, Trade Policy Research Centre, 1982.

17. Richard Senti, "Protectionism in International Insurance Transactions," <u>Intereconomics</u>, September/October 1986.

18. Bernard Wasow, "Technology Transfer in the Insurance Industry," in R.K. Shelp et al, <u>Service Industries and Economic Development</u>, Praeger 1984.

19. Olubunmi Okediji, "Government Participation in the Nigerian Insurance Market," <u>Journal of World Trade Law</u>, Vol. 20, No. 5, 1986.

20. Yoon Je Cho, "Developing Country Strategy for International Trade in Financial Services: Lessons from the opening of the Korean Insurance Market," mimeo, July 1987.

21. Christopher Findlay and Peter Forsyth, "Trade in Air Transport and Tourism Services," mimeo, October 1986. Paper prepared for 16th PAFTAD Conference. Wellington, New Zealand. January 1987.

22. Based on data from World Tourism Organisation (WTO).

23. A study of the economic benefits and costs from an increase in international tourism is contained in <u>Economic Effects of International Tourism</u>, Centre for International Economics, Canberra 1988.

24. Greg Seow, Ken Tucker, Mark Sundberg, <u>ASEAN-Australian Trade in Tourist Services</u>, ASEAN-Australia Economic Papers No. 11, 1984. The impact of tourism is measured on the demand side, allocating tourism expenditure to the various categories of final demand. Estimates cover both first-round direct effects of tourism expenditure (for example, the value-added generated by retail purchases of clothing souvenirs) as well as indirect secondary effects (for example, intermediate inputs from textile manufacture). For a discussion of the use, and limitations of input-output analysis in services see UNCTAD "Services and the Development Process", TD/B/1008 Rev. 1, 1985, paragraph 58.

25. R.H. Green, "Toward Planning Tourism in African Countries," in E. de Kadt, <u>Tourism - Passport to Development?</u>, World Bank and UNESCO, 1979.

26. E. Philip English, <u>The Great Escape: An Examination of North-South Tourism</u>, The North-South Institute, Ottawa, 1986.

27. United Nations Centre on Transnational Corporations, <u>Transnational Corporations in International Tourism</u>, 1982.

28. <u>Financial Times</u>, 10 December 1987.

29.   Chia Lin Sien and Keith Trace, "Trade and Investment in Shipping Services," mimeo, January 1987. Paper prepared for 16th PAFTAD Conference. Wellington, New Zealand. January 1987; and Sapir op cit.

30.   OECD, Maritime Transport 1986.

31.   J.A. Zerby, "On the Practicality of the UNCTAD Code for Liner Conferences," Maritime Policy and Management, 6(4) 1979.

32.   Hans Böhme, "World Shipping in Need of a More Liberal Framework," Trade Policy Research Centre, 1984.

33.   United Nations Centre on Transnational Corporations, "Transnational Corporations in the Shipping Industry: The Case of Bauxite/Alumina," (E/C. 10/T1982/14).

34.   Elliot Schrier, "Internationl Maritime Transport Services: The Outlook for Liberalisation," Trade Policy Research Centre, 1984.

35.   Modwel et al, op cit.

36.   C. Oman, Ed., New Forms of Overseas Investment by Developing Countries, OECD, 1986.

37.   Sooyong Kim, "The Korean Construction Industry as an Exporter of Services," mimeo, April 1987. Prepared for World Bank conference "Developing Countries' Interests and International Transactions in Services". Washington. July 1987.

38.   Engineering News Record, 7 July 1988 and 4 August 1988.

39.   Carliene Brenner and Celik Kurdoglu, Mastering Technology: Engineering Services Firms in Developing Countries, OECD 1988.

40.   Based on material from SELA (Secretariat of the Latin American Economic System).

41.   Brenner, op cit.

42.   "Capacity of the Engineering Industry in Colombia," in A.S. Bhalla, Technology and Employment in Industry, International Labour Office, 1985; J.C. Stephenson, "Technology Transfer by the Bechtel Organization" in R.K. Shelp et al, Services Industries and Economic Development, 1984; A. Araoz, Ed., Consulting and Engineering Design in Developing Countries, International Development Research Centre, Ottawa, 1981.

43.   Stephenson, op cit.

44.   The Services Barometer, European Service Industries Forum, No. 10, December 1987.

45.   For further discussion see Peat, Marwick, Mitchell & Co., "A Typology of Barriers to Trade in Services,: July 1986, pages 134, 142; Frank A. Rossi, "Government Impediments and Professional Constraints on the

Operations of International Accounting Organisations," The University of Chicago Legal Forum, 1986, page 159; United Nation's Centre on Transnational Corporations, "Transnational Corporations in Advertising," ST/CTC/8.

46. Geza Feketekuty, "Trade in Professional Services: An Overview," The University of Chicago Legal Forum, 1986.

47. Rossi, op cit.

48. Thierry Noyelle and Anna Dutka, International Trade in Business Services: Accounting, Advertising, Law and Management Consulting, American Enterprise Institute/Ballinger 1988.

49. Rossi, op cit.

50. Jagdish Bhagwati, "Services," in The Uruguay Round: A Handbook on the Multilateral Trade Negotiations, World Bank, 1987.

51. United Nations Centre on Transnational Corporations, "Transnational Corporations and Transborder Data Flows," ST/CTC/23, 1982.

52. Canadian National Study on Services, 1984, page 42.

53. R.J. Saunders, J.J. Warford and B. Wellenius, Telecommunications and Economic Development, for World Bank, 1983.

54. Eduardo Barrera, "Advanced Telecommunications Between Mexico and Texas: The Example of Maquiladora Programs", for Texas Department of Commerce, November 1988. For a discussion of how LDC governments frequently regard their telecommunications monopolies primarily as a source of employment and revenue see Jonathan Aronson, "The Service Industries: Growth, Trade and Development Prospects" in Growth, Exports and Jobs in a Changing World Economy, Overseas Development Council, 1988.

55. Financial Times, 6 May 1987.

56. Fernando de Mateo, "A Comparison of Data Services in Brazil and Mexico," mimeo, February 1988. Paper prepared for seminar on "Services and Development", UNCTC and Government of Peru. Lima. February 1988. See also Pablo T. Spiller, "The Political Economy of Brazilian Regulation of Transborder Data Flows," mimeo, July 1987. Paper prepared for World Bank conference "Developing Countries' Interests and International Transactions in Services". Washington. July 1987.

57. Improving International Rules of the Game, Theme III of High Level Meeting of the Committee for Information, Computer and Communications Policy. OECD. 1987.

58. R.M. Pecchioli, The Internationalisation of Banking: The Policy Issues, OECD, 1983, page 51.

59. For further discussion see P. Wellons, D. Germidis and B. Glavanis, Banks and Specialised Financial Intermediaries in Development, OECD Development Centre, 1986.

60. D. Germidis and C-A. Michalet, op cit. (Covering Argentina, Brazil, Egypt, India, Ivory Coast, Republic of Korea, Lebanon, Mexico, Peru, Philippines and Singapore).

61. United States Department of the Treasury, Report to the Congress on Foreign Government Treatment of United States Commercial Banking Organisations, op cit. This document has been subject to two revisions, in 1984 and 1986, in respect of 18 selected banking markets. It is reported that in the countries where national treatment problems remained, overall conditions "improved somewhat" between 1979 and 1984, and between 1984 and 1986, reflecting sporadic and slow improvements in treatment. In the 1986 revision, Korea and Taiwan were noted as having taken steps to liberalise their banking sectors.

62. OECD, Trends in Banking in OECD Countries, 1985, page 56.

63. Ingo Walter, Barriers to Trade in Banking and Financial Services, Trade Policy Research Centre, 1985, page 114.

64. See Abdul Z.A. Ali Insurance Development in the Arab World, 1985, page 9; Michael T. Skully, ASEAN Financial Cooperation, 1985, page 134; and Ecole Internationale de Bordeaux, Les Assurances en Afrique Francophone, 1977, page 5.

65. "The Changing Face of the International Insurance Business", Multinational Business, No. 3, 1981. It should be noted, however, that the impression of diminished presence of foreign insurers in developing countries may have been exaggerated by a process of company rationalisation. Thus, while participants in the insurance industry are still fairly numerous and diversified, there has been a tendency for a number of years in many countries towards mergers of insurance companies.

66. Emile Karaïliev, "L'Assurance Française dans le Monde", Problèmes Economiques, 3rd December 1986.

67. United Nations Centre on Transnational Corporations (UNCTC), "Transnational Reinsurance Operations", ST/CTC/15, 1980, paragraph 67.

68. UNCTAD, "Statistical survey on insurance and reinsurance operations in developing countries", TD/B/C.3/220, 14th January 1987, paragraph 26.

69. UNCTAD, "Invisibles: Insurance, Reinsurance Security", TD/B/C.3/221, February 1987, paragraph 13.

70. Compagnie Suisse de Réassurances, "L'assurance mondiale en 1985", Sigma, No. 5, May 1987.

71. UNCTAD, "Insurance in developing countries: developments in 1984-1985", op cit., paragraph 2.

72. Yoon Je Cho, "Developing Country Strategy for International Trade in Financial Services - Lessons from the opening of the Korean Insurance Market". Paper prepared for World Bank conference on Developing Countries' Interests and International Transactions in Services, Washington, July 1987.

73. Financial Times, 20th July 1987, and the Economist, 6th June 1987.

74. Proceedings of the UNCTAD, First Session, Vol. I, Final Act and Report, Annex A.IV.23, 1964.

75. UNCTAD, "Insurance in the context of services and the development process", TD/B/1014, op cit., paragraph 17.

76. United States National Study on Trade in Services, December 1983, page 225.

77. UNCTAD, TD/B/1014, op. cit., paragraph 43.

78. Drawn, variously, from S.K. Modwel, K.N. Mehrotra and S. Kumar, Trade in Services, Indian Institute for Foreign Trade, op cit., page 240; Ali, op. cit., page 211; and Skully, op. cit., page 139.

79. Annex A.IV.23 of UNCTAD I, op. cit.

80. United States National Study, op. cit., page 226.

81. See UNCTAD, TD/B/1014, op. cit., paragraph 57; Les Assurances en Afrique Francophone, op. cit., page 10; and Ali, op. cit., page 40.

82. Peter Hazell, Carlos Pomareda and Alberto Valdés, Crop Insurance for Agricultural Development, 1986, page 262.

83. Modwel et al, op. cit. page 157.

84. UNCTAD, "The Promotion of Risk Management in Developing Countries", TD/B/C.3/218, 14th January 1987, paragraph 13.

85. UNCTAD, TD/B/1014, op. cit., paragraph 59.

86. Drawn, respectively, from Skully, op. cit., page 14; and UNCTAD, TD/B/C.3/222, op. cit., paragraph 48.

87. UNCTAD "Services and the Development Process", TD/B/1008/Rev. 1, paragraph 141.

88. United Nations Centre on Transnational Corporations, Transnational Corporations in International Tourism, 1982.

89.   S.I. Papadopoulos, "World Tourism: an Economic Analysis", *Revue de tourisme*, No. 1, 1987, Table 1.

90.   Edward Dommen, *Invisible Exports from Islands*, UNCTAD Discussion Paper No. 9, page 7.

91.   United States National Study on Trade in Services, December 1983, page 260.

92.   Drawn from: World Tourism Organisation. Report of Facilitation Committee, FAL/6/7, 13th November 1986, pages 6 and 7; and Ministry of Trade and Industry, Republic of Singapore, *The Singapore Economy: New Directions*, February 1986, page 195.

93.   P. Selwyn et al, *Employment and Poverty in the Seychelles*, 1980.

94.   Greg Seow, Ken Tucker, Mark Sundberg, *ASEAN-Australian Trade in Tourist Services*, op cit. Detailed studies suggest that import content tends to decline as the level of development of a country increases. See E. Philip English, op cit., page 26.

95.   United States National Study, op cit, USTR inventory, page 14.

96.   C. Tisdell, *Tourism, the Environment, International Trade and Public Economics*, ASEAN-Australia Economic Papers No. 6, 1984, page 20, drawing on R. Daroesman, *An Economic Survey of Bali*, Bulletin of Indonesian Economic Studies, 9(3), 1973.

97.   English, op cit., page 21.

98.   G.M. Arroyo, *The Services Sector in the Philippines*, ASEAN-Australia Working Paper No. 2, 1984, page 29.

99.   Sieh Lee Mei Ling, *The Services Sector in Malaysia*, ASEAN-Australia Working Paper No. 8, 1984, page 33.

100.   See UNCTAD, "Shipping in the Context of Services and the Development Process", TD/B/1013, 9th November 1984, paragraph 23.

101.   For further discussion, see Australian Bureau of Transport Economics, *Cargo Centralisation in the Overseas Liner Trades*, 1982.

102.   For further discussion, see Charles Drury and Peter Stokes, *Ship Finance: the Credit Crisis*, Lloyds Shipping Economist Study, 1983.

103.   OECD, *Maritime Transport 1988*. (Forthcoming)

104.   Chia Lin Sien and Keith Trace, "Trade and Investment in Shipping Services", op cit., page 10.

105. UN, Department of International Economic and Social Affairs, "Main Issues in Transport for Developing Countries during the Third United Nations Development Decade 1981-1990", ST/ESA/117, 1982, page 9; and Department of Foreign Affairs and Trade, "Australian Traded Services", Canberra. 1987, page 66.

106. United Nations Centre on Transnational Corporations (UNCTC), "Transnational Corporations in the Shipping Industry: The Case of Bauxite/Alumina", (E/C.10/1982/14).

107. OECD, Maritime Transport 1986, page 127.

108. Lawrence J. White, "International Trade in Ocean Shipping Services: The United States and the World", mimeo for American Enterprise Institute, page 231.

109. UNCTAD, TD/B/1013, op cit., paragraph 57.

110. I.M. Sinan, "UNCTAD and Flags of convenience", Journal of World Trade Law, March-April 1984.

111. UNCTAD, TD/B/1013, op cit., paragraph 50.

112. UNCTAD, TD/B/1013, op cit., paragraph 149.

113. A.J. Yeats, Trade and Development Policies, Macmillan 1981; and "Ocean Freight Rates and their effects on Exports of Developing Countries", UNCTAD/ST/SHIP/11, 17th November 1987.

114. Chia, op cit., page 10.

115. S.K. Modwel, K.N. Mehrotra, S. Kumar, op cit.

116. Sinan, op cit., page 100.

117. UNCTAD, TD/B/1013, op cit., paragraph 81.

118. For further discussion, see Chia, op cit.

119. UNCTAD, TD/B/1013, op cit., paragraph 53.

120. The inclusion of labour services, as well as raising major policy implications also gives rise to the statistical issue of distinguishing "labour income" (included in the IMF "services" category) from "migrant transfers" and "workers' remittances" (which, as relating to earnings of those who stay in an economy for a year or more, are, under IMF criteria, excluded).

121. This is demonstrated in a series of case studies for the Republic of Korea, Brazil, the Philippines and Argentina, in A. Araoz, op cit.

122. See, World Bank, The Construction Industry: Issues and Strategies in Developing Countries, 1984, page 40.

123. C.W. Stahl, ASEAN's Trade in Labour Services, ASEAN-Australia Working Papers, No. 1, 1984.

124. Engineering News Record, 7th August 1986.

125. Engineering News Record, 17th July 1986.

126. UNCTAD, "Services and the Development Process", TD/B/1008/Rev.1, paragraph 212.

127. Canadian National Study on Services, January 1984, page 31.

128. Bohn-Young Koo, "Korea: A Leader in Turnkey Projects", in C. Oman, New Forms of Overseas Investment by Developing Countries. OECD 1986, page 106.

129. Araoz, op cit., page 11; and "Capacity of the Engineering Industry in Colombia", Institute of Technological Research, Bogota, in A.S. Bhalla, op cit.

130. World Bank, op cit., page 97.

131. Sanjaya Lall, "India: A Major South-South Investor", in Oman, op cit., page 50.

132. Kemal Abdallah-Khodja, "Algeria's Experience with New International Investment Relations", in C. Oman, Ed., New Forms of International Investment in Developing Countries, OECD, 1984.

133. This question has been discussed extensively by Jagdish Bhagwati. See, for example, "Trade in Services and Developing Countries", Xth Annual Geneva Lecture, London School of Economics, 1985.

134. M.I. Arbella, "Les Migrations de Travailleurs d'Asie du Sud et du Sud-Est", Problèmes Economiques, 5th December 1984.

135. United Nations Centre on Transnational Corporations, "Role of Transnational Corporations in Services, Including Transborder Data Flows," E/C.10/1987/11, 26 January 1987, paragraph 35.

136. Myron Weiner, "International Migration and Development: Indians in the Persian Gulf," Population and Development Review, March 1982, page 3.

137. OECD, Competition Policy and the Professions, 1985, paragraph 6.

138. The following observations are drawn from Thierry Noyelle and Anna Dutka, op cit.

139. Frank A. Rossi, op cit., page 141; and United States "National Study on Trade in Services", December 1983.

140. For further discussion, see Mario Kakabadse, <u>International Trade in Services: Prospects for Liberalisation in the 1990s</u>, the Atlantic Institute for International Affairs, 1987; Government of Singapore, <u>The Singapore Economy: New Directions</u>, February 1986, page 189; and Dorothy Riddle, <u>Service-Led Growth: The Role of the Service Sector in World Development</u>, Praeger 1986.

141. Weiner, op cit.

142. OECD, "Expert Meeting on 'Migration and Development' held at the Development Centre, 17th to 19th February 1987," Summary Report, 20 March 1987.

143. OECD, "Conference d'experts nationaux sur l'avenir des migrations," 13th to 15th May 1986.

144. Rossi, op cit., page 157.

145. Julian Arkell and Ian S. Harrison, "A Sectoral Study on the Relevance of the OECD Conceptual Framework to International Trade in Consultancy Services," May 1987.

146. OECD, <u>Competition Policy and the Professions</u>, op cit. paragraphs 131 to 144.

147. See, for example, Alfredio Juinio, "What the Client Requires of the Consulting Engineer" and Alimullah Khan and S.M. Shahidullah, "Problems faced by the Consulting Engineering Profession in Bangladesh" in <u>The Role of the Consulting Engineer in Development Projects and the Transfer of Technology to Developing Countries</u>, Federation international des ingenieurs-conseils (FIDIC), 1979.

148. United National Centre on Transnational Corporations, "Transnational Corporations in Advertising," ST/CTC/8.

149. For further discussion of definitional questions, see <u>Telecommunication Network-Based Services: Implications for Policy</u>, ICCP Series, Number 18. OECD 1989.

150. For further discussion of the impact of ICC services on forms of trade, see UNCTAD, "Service and the Development Process: Further Studies", TD/B/1100, 2nd July 1986, paragraph 39; G. Feketekuty and K. Hauser, <u>Information Technology and Trade in Services</u>, Economic Impact 1985/4; and J. Rada, "Information Technology and Services", mimeo. 1986, quoted in R.J. Krommenacker, "The Impact of Information Technology on Trade Interdependence", <u>Journal of World Trade Law</u>, July/August 1986.

151. <u>The Emerging Global Information Economy: A Three Year Research Program</u>, Centre européen de prospective et de synthèse, PROMETHEE, December 1986.

152. Drawn from S. Macdonald and T. Mandeville, "Telecommunications in ASEAN and Australia", ASEAN-Australia Economic Paper No. 5, 1984, page 17; and Telecommunications Industry Research Centre forecasts, in the Financial Times, 19th October 1987.

153. The linkage effects of ICC services are dealt with in a number of papers from the United Nations Centre on Transnational Corporations (UNCTC) which have been drawn on in preparing this Chapter. They include "Transnational Corporations and Transborder Data Flows: A Technical Paper", ST/CTC/23, 1982; "Transborder Data Flows: Access to the International On-line Data-base Market", ST/CTC/41, 1983; "International Trade and Foreign Direct Investment in Data Services: Transborder Data Flows in the context of Services and the Development Process", TD/B/1016, August 1984; "Role of Transnational Corporations in Services, including Transborder Data Flows", E/C.10/1987/11, 26th January 1987.

154. Country data drawn from "Scientific and Technological Information for Development", United Nations Centre for Science and Technology for Development, 1985.

155. Telecommunications Policies: Experiences and Challenges, Theme II of High Level Meeting of the Committee for Information, Computer and Communications Policy. OECD 1987.

156. The Internationalisation of Software and Computer Services, ICCP Series, Number 17. OECD 1989.

157. F.M. Greguras (Fenwick, Davis and West), mimeo, 6th January 1987

158. Special Secretariat of Informatics, Government of Brazil, "Transborder Data Flows and Brazil", study prepared for UNCTC, 1983.

159. International Telecommunication Union, "The Missing Link" in documentation submitted in GATT.

160. For further discussion of "centralisation" concerns, see P. Cotrim, "L'informatique au Brésil" in Informatique, Coopération Internationale et Indépendance, Documentation française, 1980, page 54.

161. Pablo T. Spiller, op cit.

162. UNIDO, "Informatics for Industrial Development", 1985, page 26.

163. "Transborder Data Flows and Brazil", op cit.

164. Spiller, op cit.

WHERE TO OBTAIN OECD PUBLICATIONS
OÙ OBTENIR LES PUBLICATIONS DE L'OCDE

ARGENTINA – ARGENTINE
Carlos Hirsch S.R.L.,
Galería Guemes, Florida 165, 4° Piso,
1333 Buenos Aires
    Tel. 30.7122, 331.1787 y 331.2391
Telegram.: Hirsch-Baires

AUSTRALIA – AUSTRALIE
D.A. Book (Aust.) Pty. Ltd.
11-13 Station Street (P.O. Box 163)
Mitcham, Vic. 3132   Tel. (03) 873 4411
Telex: AA37911 DA BOOK   Telefax: (03)873.5679

AUSTRIA – AUTRICHE
OECD Publications and Information Centre,
4 Simrockstrasse,
5300 Bonn (Germany)   Tel. (0228) 21.60.45
Telex: 8 86300 Bonn   Telefax: (0228)26.11.04
Gerold & Co., Graben 31, Wien 1   Tel. (1)533.50.14

BELGIUM – BELGIQUE
Jean de Lannoy, Avenue du Roi 202
B-1060 Bruxelles   Tel. (02) 538.51.69/538.08.41
Telex: 63220

CANADA
Renouf Publishing Company Ltd
1294 Algoma Road, Ottawa, Ont. K1B 3W8
    Tel: (613) 741-4333
Telex: 053-4783   Telefax: (613)741.5439
Stores:
61 Sparks St., Ottawa, Ont. K1P 5R1
    Tel: (613) 238-8985
211 rue Yonge St., Toronto, Ont. M5B 1M4
    Tel: (416) 363-3171
Federal Publications Inc.,
165 University Avenue,
Toronto, ON M5H 3B9   Tel. (416)581-1552
Telefax: (416)581.1743
Les Publications Fédérales
1185 rue de l'Université
Montréal, PQ H3B 1R7   Tel.(514)954.1633
Les Éditions la Liberté Inc.,
3020 Chemin Sainte-Foy,
Sainte-Foy, P.Q. G1X 3V6,   Tel. (418)658-3763
Telefax: (418)658.3763

DENMARK – DANEMARK
Munksgaard Export and Subscription Service
35, Nørre Søgade, P.O. Box 212148
DK-1016 København K   Tel. (45 1)12.85.70
Telex: 19431 MUNKS DK   Telefax: (45 1)12.93.87

FINLAND – FINLANDE
Akateeminen Kirjakauppa,
Keskuskatu 1, P.O. Box 128
00100 Helsinki   Tel. (358 0)12141
Telex: 125080   Telefax: (358 0)121.4441

FRANCE
OCDE/OECD
Mail Orders/Commandes par correspondance :
2, rue André-Pascal,
75775 Paris Cedex 16   Tel. (1) 45.24.82.00
Bookshop/Librairie : 33, rue Octave-Feuillet
75016 Paris
    Tel. (1) 45.24.81.67 ou/ou (1) 45.24.81.81
Telex: 620 160 OCDE   Telefax: (33-1)45.24.85.00
Librairie de l'Université,
12a, rue Nazareth,
13602 Aix-en-Provence   Tel. 42.26.18.08

GERMANY – ALLEMAGNE
OECD Publications and Information Centre,
4 Simrockstrasse,
5300 Bonn   Tel. (0228) 21.60.45
Telex: 8 86300 Bonn   Telefax: (0228)26.11.04

GREECE – GRÈCE
Librairie Kauffmann,
28, rue du Stade, 105 64 Athens   Tel. 322.21.60
Telex: 218187 LIKA Gr

HONG KONG
Government Information Services,
Publications (Sales) Office,
Information Services Department
No. 1, Battery Path, Central
Tel.(5)23.31.91   Telex: 802.61190

ICELAND – ISLANDE
Mál Mog Menning
Laugavegi 18, Pósthólf 392
121 Reykjavik   Tel. 15199/24240

INDIA – INDE
Oxford Book and Stationery Co.,
Scindia House,
New Delhi 110001   Tel. 331.5896/5308
Telex: 31 61990 AM IN   Telefax: (11) 332.5993
17 Park St., Calcutta 700016   Tel. 240832

INDONESIA – INDONÉSIE
Pdii-Lipi, P.O. Box 3065/JKT.
Jakarta   Tel. 583467
Telex: 73 45875

IRELAND – IRLANDE
TDC Publishers - Library Suppliers,
12 North Frederick Street,
Dublin 1   Tel. 744835-749677
Telex: 33530TDCP EI Telefax: 748416

ITALY – ITALIE
Libreria Commissionaria Sansoni,
Via Benedetto Fortini 120/10,
Casella Post. 552
50125 Firenze   Tel. (055)645415
Telex: 570466   Telefax: (39.55)641257
Via Bartolini 29, 20155 Milano   Tel. 365083
La diffusione delle pubblicazioni OCSE viene assicurata
dalle principali librerie ed anche da :
Editrice e Libreria Herder,
Piazza Montecitorio 120, 00186 Roma
Tel. 6794628   Telex: NATEL I 621427
Libreria Hœpli,
Via Hœpli 5, 20121 Milano   Tel. 865446
Telex:31.33.95   Telefax: (39.2)805.2886
Libreria Scientifica
Dott. Lucio de Biasio "Aeiou"
Via Meravigli 16, 20123 Milano   Tel. 807679
Telefax: 800175

JAPAN – JAPON
OECD Publications and Information Centre,
Landic Akasaka Building, 2-3-4 Akasaka,
Minato-ku, Tokyo 107   Tel. 586.2016
    Telefax: (81.3) 584.7929

KOREA – CORÉE
Kyobo Book Centre Co. Ltd.
P.O.Box 1658, Kwang Hwa Moon
Seoul   Tel. (REP) 730.78.91
Telefax: 735.0030

MALAYSIA/SINGAPORE – MALAISIE/SINGAPOUR
University of Malaya Co-operative Bookshop Ltd.,
P.O. Box 1127, Jalan Pantai Baru 59100
Kuala Lumpur, Malaysia/Malaisie
Tel. 756.5000/756.5425   Telefax: 757.3661
Information Publications Pte Ltd
Pei-Fu Industrial Building,
24 New Industrial Road No. 02-06
Singapore/Singapour 1953   Tel. 283.1786/283.1798
Telefax: 284.8875

NETHERLANDS – PAYS-BAS
SDU Uitgeverij
Christoffel Plantijnstraat 2
Postbus 20014
2500 EA's-Gravenhage   Tel. (070)78.99.11
Voor bestellingen: Tel. (070)78.98.80
Telex: 32486 stdru   Telefax: (070)47.63.51

NEW ZEALAND – NOUVELLE-ZÉLANDE
Government Printing Office Bookshops:
Auckland: Retail Bookshop, 25 Rutland Street,
Mail Orders, 85 Beach Road
Private Bag C.P.O.
Hamilton: Retail: Ward Street,
Mail Orders, P.O. Box 857
Wellington: Retail, Mulgrave Street, (Head Office)
Telex: COVPRNT NZ 31370   Telefax: (04)734943
Cubacade World Trade Centre,
Mail Orders, Private Bag
Christchurch: Retail, 159 Hereford Street,
Mail Orders, Private Bag
Dunedin: Retail, Princes Street,
Mail Orders, P.O. Box 1104

NORWAY – NORVÈGE
Narvesen Info Center – NIC,
Bertrand Narvesens vei 2,
P.O.B. 6125 Etterstad, 0602 Oslo 6
    Tel. (02)67.83.10/(02)68.40.20
Telex: 79668 NIC N   Telefax: (47 2)68.53.47

PAKISTAN
Mirza Book Agency
65 Shahrah Quaid-E-Azam, Lahore 3   Tel. 66839
Telegram: "Knowledge"

PORTUGAL
Livraria Portugal, Rua do Carmo 70-74,
1117 Lisboa Codex   Tel. 347.49.82/3/4/5

SINGAPORE/MALAYSIA – SINGAPOUR/MALAISIE
See "Malaysia/Singapore". Voir «Malaisie/Singapour»

SPAIN – ESPAGNE
Mundi-Prensa Libros, S.A.,
Castelló 37, Apartado 1223,
Madrid-28001   Tel. 431.33.99
Telex: 49370 MPLI   Telefax: 275.39.98
Librería Bosch, Ronda Universidad 11,
Barcelona 7   Tel. 317.53.08/317.53.58

SWEDEN – SUÈDE
Fritzes Fackboksföretaget
Box 16356, S 103 27 STH,
Regeringsgatan 12,
DS Stockholm   Tel. (08)23.89.00
Telex: 12387   Telefax: (08)20.50.21
Subscription Agency/Abonnements:
Wennergren-Williams AB,
Box 30004, S104 25 Stockholm   Tel. (08)54.12.00
Telex: 19937   Telefax: (08)50.82.86

SWITZERLAND – SUISSE
OECD Publications and Information Centre,
4 Simrockstrasse,
5300 Bonn (Germany)   Tel. (0228) 21.60.45
Telex: 8 86300 Bonn   Telefax: (0228)26.11.04
Librairie Payot,
6 rue Grenus, 1211 Genève 11   Tel. (022)731.89.50
Telex: 28356
Maditec S.A.
Ch. des Palettes 4
1020 – Renens/Lausanne   Tel. (021)635.08.65
Telefax: (021)635.07.80
United Nations Bookshop/Librairie des Nations-Unies
Palais des Nations, 1211 – Geneva 10
    Tel. (022)734.60.11 (ext. 48.72)
Telex: 289696 (Attn: Sales)   Telefax: (022)733.98.79

TAIWAN – FORMOSE
Good Faith Worldwide Int'l Co., Ltd.
9th floor, No. 118, Sec.2, Chung Hsiao E. Road
Taipei   Tel. 391.7396/391.7397
Telefax: 394.9176

THAILAND – THAILANDE
Suksit Siam Co., Ltd., 1715 Rama IV Rd.,
Samyam, Bangkok 5   Tel. 2511630

TURKEY – TURQUIE
Kültur Yayinlari Is-Türk Ltd. Sti.
Atatürk Bulvari No. 191/Kat. 21
Kavaklidere/Ankara   Tel. 25.07.60
Dolmabahce Cad. No. 29
Besiktas/Istanbul   Tel. 160.71.88
Telex: 43482B

UNITED KINGDOM – ROYAUME-UNI
H.M. Stationery Office   (01)873-8483
Postal orders only:
P.O.B. 276, London SW8 5DT
Telephone orders: (01) 873-9090, or
Personal callers:
49 High Holborn, London WC1V 6HB
Telex:297138   Telefax: 873.8463
Branches at: Belfast, Birmingham, Edinburgh,
Manchester

UNITED STATES – ÉTATS-UNIS
OECD Publications and Information Centre,
2001 L Street, N.W., Suite 700,
Washington, D.C. 20036-4095   Tel. (202)785.6323
Telex:440245 WASHINGTON D.C.
Telefax: (202)785.0350

VENEZUELA
Libreria del Este,
Avda F. Miranda 52, Aptdo. 60337,
Edificio Galipan, Caracas 106
    Tel. 951.1705/951.2307/951.1297
Telegram: Libreste Caracas

YUGOSLAVIA – YOUGOSLAVIE
Jugoslovenska Knjiga, Knez Mihajlova 2,
P.O.B. 36, Beograd   Tel. 621.992
Telex: 12466 jk bgd

Orders and inquiries from countries where Distributors
have not yet been appointed should be sent to: OECD,
Publications Service, 2, rue André-Pascal, 75775 PARIS
CEDEX 16.

Les commandes provenant de pays où l'OCDE n'a pas
encore désigné de distributeur devraient être adressées à :
OCDE, Service des Publications. 2, rue André-Pascal,
75775 PARIS CEDEX 16.

72547-6-1989

OECD PUBLICATIONS, 2, rue André-Pascal, 75775 PARIS CEDEX 16 - No. 44927 1989
PRINTED IN FRANCE
(22 89 01 1) ISBN 92-64-13278-3